Beth,
Hope this brings
you a few hours of
fun + laughs -
Happy Reading!
Bonnie

Maternally Speaking

I Gave Birth To Four Eggs!
(One Scrambled, Fried, Over Easy & Sunny Side Up)

BONNIE LOWELL

Maternally Speaking: I Gave Birth To Four Eggs
(One Scrambled, Fried, Over Easy & Sunny Side Up)

Bonnie Lowell

ISBN: 978-1-936214-09-9

Library of Congress Control Number: 2010921418

Published by My Life Is An Open Book, an Imprint of Wyatt-MacKenzie

My Life Is An Open Book
An Imprint of Wyatt-MacKenzie

Wyatt-MacKenzie Publishing
DEADWOOD, OREGON

www.wyattmackenzie.com

DEDICATION

I owe a debt of gratitude to my mother and mentor, Arlene Hanrahan, who has taught me that there are few boundaries. She is compassionate, considerate and is overflowing with an abundance of patience, tolerance and warm humor. She is a tough act to follow but should be the measurement of decency to which all women should strive to achieve. She deserves the ultimate Certificate of Hormonal Excellence!

Live,

If it were not for my plentiful ovaries that provided me with my brood: Ryan, Nicki, Brad and Alex, for whom I feel immense love and pride, I wouldn't have had nearly as much fun, excitement or purpose in my life. Our mutual love, respect and support creates an invaluable friendship.

Love,

I am so grateful for my fiancé, Kris Johnson, who is my calm and reliable rock. He has given me loving support and unquestionable encouragement. Our lives are filled with continual laughter and contentment which has finally put me in my happy place!

Laugh!

CONTENTS

INTRODUCTION

We Are the Ovarian Club!

In my opinion, being a woman means having an abundance of choice. And I think we would all agree that having many options is a great thing. We've been given the reputation of having a sixth sense, astute hearing and investigative skills, a woman's intuition and eyes in the back of our heads. We hold the prerogative to change our minds whenever convenient. It's awesome! I surely get my money's worth out of that one!

We can say we have a headache to get out of compromising positions and use pregnancy to avoid strenuous work or skimpy clothing. We invented hand-slapping of frisky paws and the words "I'm not in the mood" can be our convenient repellent to just about anything. Although usually we don't earn an equal day's compensation, most women I know (myself included) have a bit of control freakishness in them and regardless, would truly prefer to be *in charge* anyway. Is it really such a big deal that we don't have equivalent equipment or share the ease of being able to urinate in the woods on a whim? I think it's an even trade, don't you?

I have shimmied my way into many a group of men gathered around the engine of a car with their heads tucked under the raised hood, totally comfortable discussing calibration of timing or revving a carburetor just for effect. I could repack my own wheel bearings if I was pressed to. Yet, on another day, I can play the damsel in distress, if I prefer to avoid lying on a creeper and getting transmission fluid drippings on my earrings. I have the opportunity to get as dirty and grimy as *one of the guys,* then put on some makeup, something frilly, smelling like the sweetest gardenia and teeter around on heels that will get me all the male attention I want. It's really the best of both worlds!

Trust me, you can stack up bonus (man) points if you can load and shoot your own shotgun, spit chewing tobacco, sink an eight ball with precision, drink like a pirate, name all of the NFL teams and can hold your own like a roughed-up hockey player. And quite frankly, if you are willing to do any or all of these things in a bikini, you'll have gained more male bonding than you'll know what to do with. But, let's be honest, they really weren't expecting us to be good at any of those things. So it's worth extra points when we are, and I'll bet the real bikini image won't match the one that's in their head anyway!

All kidding aside, all my life I have surrounded myself with extraordinarily strong and independent women who didn't need a push-up bra to make their point. Many relatives, friends and colleagues have served as perfect examples of the smart woman who persevered to become great role models and providers for their family's needs, both with financial reward and emotional stability. I am proud to know this collection of silent feminists—consisting of subtle leaders and loving caregivers—teaching wisdom, great family values, faith and decency. Many of them don't feel worthy of wearing a cloak with iridescent letters on it which reads: **Super-woman**. Regardless, many of them deserve one!

Having the support of my Ovarian Club has allowed me to exude a comedic aura around me which propels my sense of humor. In turn it gives me the ability to laugh in the face of challenge and adversity, along with a positive outlook to conquer the most dismal situations and a humorous appreciation for the absurdity that life dishes out. Laughter is some of the best medicine, and combined with hugs, the extremely therapeutic results are endless.

Within the first three weeks of a human conception our destiny is predetermined and carefully mapped out. We had a 50/50 chance of becoming either a male or a female. The ultimate innie or outie! Our genetics were swayed, DNA decided and our gender was irrefutably molded. Most of us women believe we had good fortune in becoming an Ovarian Club member. Yes. There are definite trials and tribulations that go along with being a woman and the hormonal fluctuation is extreme. There are distinct characteristics, attitudes and developmental growth bestowed on women alone—which make us unusually complex and unique beings. Plus there is relief that, thank goodness, we weren't stuck with ridiculous male genitalia. I am very thankful for that, alone!

I call these stages the Seven Wonders of Womanhood, during which we form the feminine bond that creates a resiliency beyond duplication.

1. **Breasts:** Like other extraordinary monumental structures, we possess breasts which give us a distinct purpose while offering a breathtaking landscape.

2. **Shaving:** Our obsession with hair removal is proof of our devotion to and continual maintenance of the feminine form.

3. **Weight:** Fluctuating weight for most women becomes an unrelenting battle to reduce the bulge, for the sake of self-improvement and to maintain our dignity.

4. **Menses:** It is our predictable and relentless monthly giving that prepares us for all unexpected lifecycles including impregnation, undoubtedly one of the most profound experiences.

5. **Childbirth:** It is an unselfish gift from which our strength surpasses our expectations and unconditional love is born.

6. **Motherhood:** For some, choosing to reproduce capitalizes on all of our maternal nurturing, teaching and protective skills.

7. **Menopause:** This is the final phase of balancing all of our hormonal upheaval and the ultimate celebration of womanhood!

Join me in my amusing interpretation, as I commemorate each of these seven important phases. (Long overdue congratulations are awarded to those of you who have achieved the true essence of womanhood by successfully conquering some, or all of them, yourselves!) There are no dues required to become a member of the Ovarian Club, and in your home you are automatically nominated CEO of the board. Through your membership you have gained mutual admiration and can lean on other members as long as you provide hugs and laughter in return. Based upon the most recent vote, the club has decided you are deserving of a Certificate of Hormonal Excellence and a treat (which you don't have to share with anyone)! Welcome to the club!

In the meantime, *you go girl!* Why not try to surprise him anyway. Get yourself a 20-gauge, Remington 1187 and a bottle of whiskey. Don't forget to study the roster!

NFL Teams

Arizona Cardinals	Miami Dolphins
Atlanta Falcons	Minnesota Vikings
Baltimore Ravens	New England Patriots
Buffalo Bills	New Orleans Saints
Carolina Panthers	New York Giants
Chicago Bears	New York Jets
Cincinnati Bengals	Oakland Raiders
Cleveland Browns	Philadelphia Eagles
Dallas Cowboys	Pittsburg Steelers
Denver Broncos	San Diego Chargers
Detroit Lions	San Francisco 49ers
Green Bay Packers	Seattle Seahawks
Houston Texans	St. Louis Rams
Indianapolis Colts	Tampa Bay Buccaneers
Jacksonville Jaguars	Tennessee Titans
Kansas City Chiefs	Washington Redskins

Who can't use extra bonus points?

Part 1

The Seven Wonders of Womanhood

CHAPTER 1
My Bosom Buddies

During our adolescent stage, there is little to differentiate us from the male species. This seemed especially true when I had everything going against me, like my short pixie haircut and the rugged hand-me-downs (I had to wear) from my brother. My mom should have gotten the hint every time we'd meet up with someone and, looking down at me, they would inquire about her son's age or name. I was destined to resemble and be mistaken for a boy until the fourth grade.

Finally, my budding estrogen caused swelling in my chest which was a breakthrough for my unisex identity crisis. I then felt justified in taking a stand. I had a courageous discussion with my mother, stating that many of my friends were wearing training bras and that I thought I was blooming ready to fill one myself. (I'm not exactly sure how one could train for having breasts, and why they were called "training" bras anyway? Breasts just gradually grow with you. It's not like all of a sudden Mom hands you a training bra that already has a pair of double D's in them. Whoa! Now that would take some training!)

As my mammary glands slowly developed, they did provide a new sense of identity. Eventually they extended beyond my nose and became the foremost part of me to enter a room. They couldn't help but be perky and confident when they were leading the way. I soon advanced from a one-size-fits-all to a real bra with actual cup holders. (I never have understood the method of sizing, though. Cup sizes A, B, C, D and gigantic! I think the ski clubs have come up with the closest measuring system: beginners, bunny slopes, hills, moguls and mountains. I think we could all figure out who is what, don't you think so?)

I began as many of us who bear a pair did, with one that closely resembled a cut-off t-shirt with straps. It didn't matter. It was the straps at that point that were the most important part. I just wanted everyone to notice that I had straps. The rest inside the bra was well-disguised forbidden fruit, but it was the elastic bands and clasp that made it finally apparent I was a girl, and that somewhere under there I did have the fruit to prove it!

There came a time when I realized that my bosom buddies would get me attention. Lots of boys have an automatic infatuation with them and a poor ability to conceal their obvious trance. It was powerful having a modest set of hills. *Nah nah, nah nah, nah! We've got something you can't see.* Not to say they didn't try. Much of the male puberty is spent attempting to get a peek at anything and everything they can. And I intended on keeping my girls under wraps. Frankly, so did my mother. She added rows of lace to cover the cleavage on my swimsuit, for Pete's sake! My near-turtleneck tan lines were hideous.

Then I had a terrible setback, or shall I say reprieve. It was discovered that I had scoliosis and had to have back surgery to fuse my spine. This entailed wearing a twenty-pound body cast—armor which covered my body with more effectiveness than a chastity belt. My girls were under wraps, all right! For a greater portion of seventh and eighth grades they were guarded by a half-inch-thick layer of plaster from my chin to the tops of my thighs. Once they were finally unveiled after nine long months of captivity, they were eager to bust out and be free. If it had not been for the cast stunting my growth, I may have actually made it to the gigantic category.

It didn't take long, however, before I got sick and tired of having a set of moguls. *Could you look up here, in my eyes please!* Most boys were already at a total advantage of being shorter than us females. They were at a perfect level and loving it. That's why most of them rarely complained about their height during those early teen years. The scenery was grand. And let's face it: the boys with true animal instinct could, from blocks away, detect when the tips of the iceberg were erect. It was like they had built-in sonar. At the beach, their heads would frantically poke up like gophers from their holes. Straining their busy little necks, they'd quickly distinguish the best pair and the news would travel like wildfire. *Hey guys, I* wanted to say, *there's more to us than a couple of landforms!*

After years of having my moguls around, I sometimes forget they're even there. Sometimes they feel tender, maybe as proof that they are real, with feeling and not just strategically placed fatty deposits. Occasionally they get in the way when I golf. Periodically they catch things which can either be helpful or extremely embarrassing. But the most annoying part was having to swat at adolescent males with groping hands trying to cop a feel. Those guys were so jealous they didn't have any. If they *did* have 'em, I suspect their hands might be preoccupied kneading their supple loaves much of the day.

Just when I thought I was fully developed, surprise! I became pregnant with my first child. Yowza Mama! I never dreamed I'd own a pair of mountains that looked like that. Even *I* was impressed and thought my cleavage was stunning. Then the revelation came to me that I could finally put my breasts to good use. Not that I invented the idea of expressing a frothy white beverage through my personal milk jugs and sharing it with my offspring, it just wasn't something that I had ever visualized before then. As it turned out, I breast-fed for many health and bonding benefits for my baby, but also just because I could, damn it!

Then I went through another identity crisis. All I had become was a brunette milking machine. My flesh-covered bottles were hanging out more often than they were in my blouse. They were alternately poked, kneaded, patted, fondled and even bitten on occasion. And that wasn't even by my husband. A baby's gums clamping down, during an early teething stage, are stronger than I ever would have imagined. It was enough to bring tears to my eyes and beg for mercy more than once!

During their downtime my receptacles were kept in an unflattering sling-style bra with trapdoors and combination locks (okay, I'm kidding about the locks) to conceal their valuable contents. Most romance was lost. Getting me aroused could cause a geyser. I never thought I'd resort to stuffing my bra, but I had to use circular pads to catch the overflow leakage.

My jugs released milk upon command and often-times dribbled at the sound or even the mere thought of a baby crying. On occasion the liquid embellishment began to anxiously squirt out of my chest before my open-mouthed baby could latch on. The poor thing would try to follow the stream while getting squirted in the eye. It was like a carnival game. *Crawl right up! See if you can squirt the milk in the baby's mouth without getting any on its hair, in the eyes or into the ears.* The whole thing was a sticky mess, the only prize being a peaceful baby and a half hour TV break.

The shutoff valves on my breasts seemed to be non-discriminatory. They didn't care whether it was my baby or someone else's who was in need. I would be standing in aisle #12 of the grocery store and sure enough, in aisle #4 there was a hungry baby who sensed there was fresh milk in the house. My internal faucets would let loose and my twins would start to gush. *Clean up in aisle 12!* I'd be standing there with embarrassing wet bull's-eye target stains of sappy milk seeping through my shirt while a gawking bag boy stared straight at my targets in awe. With his jaw slapping the conveyer belt, he'd mumble, "Paper or plastic?" *I'd like both; plastic to cover my leaking udders and paper for over my head. Thank you.*

Then there were the days I pumped the stuff for my baby so I could return to work. I had so much milk I put up a stand at the end of the driveway with a TV tray and money box. I fed all the kids in the neighborhood. I shouldn't have been embarrassed at the natural process of pumping milk, but the whirring sound of the mechanical pump and the suction devices which hung from my teats were much too cow-like. All that was missing was the ring in my nose and a big bell around my neck. At work, everyone seemed to clear out of the building while I did it, even though I was behind closed doors of course. It made them all a bit uncomfortable and, coincidentally, hungry for ice cream!

After those days were over, I finally was ready to relinquish my nursing duties. Weaning was quite a task. When I heard the term "dry up" I thought it would be a piece of cake. It's supply and demand—if there is no longer a demand, my body should stop producing, right? Evidently my internal milkmaid didn't get the message and kept sending it up until I was beyond full.

After three very long days of extreme discomfort, my extended skin was stretched around my grossly swollen, mountainous breasts. They almost qualified as a ski resort. I thought I would explode like a balloon from a pin-prick if I were touched. I kept them bound and gagged, but even with the gentlest pressure I could make them squirt across the room and hit the remote to change the channel on the TV.

Finally, the buffet table did dry up and all the neighborhood kids had to fend for themselves. And sad to say, some of my bosom's youthful beauty, once smooth and taut, had dried up too. They would never look or act the same after that. Poor girls! For awhile they even felt a little lost, looking down, moping around without a purpose.

Some women work to create and augment the best possible breasts they can have. Some want to expand their cup size to increase the attention they bring upon themselves. Other women reduce their bra size so there isn't so much weight to carry around. I have always accepted mine for what they are—not perfect and slightly lopsided, but I have been satisfied thus far by their performance.

I used the hell out of them; therefore my topless days are over. Any life that may have been left in them has been extinguished by the mammogram machine. Elasticity is lost, and they do get away from me now and then. Occasionally, my honey rolls on one of them, and I politely ask for it back. I can only imagine my plums will continue to prune as the years go on, but oh, the stories they can tell. There were the Mardi Gras days when men would throw strings of colorful plastic beads just to get a glimpse of my pert beauties. Now that I'm more mature and not quite as uplifted, I'm offered diamonds… to keep my blouse on!

A job at Hooters is probably out of the question, but thanks to the push-up bra, my twins may still turn a few heads. And I'm hoping they'll still get me out of a couple of speeding tickets yet, provide me with a few free drinks from adoring alcohol-induced fans, and if times get tough, at least my grandchildren will never go hungry!

Drinks in my blouse—I mean, on the house!

CHAPTER 2
Hair Today, Gone Tomorrow

I was thirteen and home alone one day, overflowing with girlish estrogen and feeling ready to explore my second wonder of womanhood. That is to say, impatience and curiosity got the best of me. I locked the bathroom door and carefully opened my mother's drawer in the vanity. I unsnapped the smooth, shimmery metal handle from its holder and daringly removed the forbidden cover that concealed its razor-sharp edge. I knew that this was a huge step into the woman's world. I'd heard that once you start you can never go back. Whatever *that* could possibly mean to a young teenager! I've always loved a dare!

Nervously I spread a generous layer of my dad's shaving cream up and down my leg. It felt cool on my skin. I began running the razor's edge from my ankle up to my knee. I was feeling so grown-up and mature until the fluffy white shaving cream began to turn pink. As I snagged small pieces of the top layer of skin I swear I exposed some nerves. Despite the burning sensation I carefully continued shaving the remainder of my leg, nicking a path up to my bony knee caps. My deep red, all-American-girl blood was surfacing and in some areas began to actually drip. Trying to keep my cool, I bravely began washing the bloody foam from my throbbing leg, and then swiftly lathered up the other leg. Boy, it didn't seem that tricky when I had seen it done on TV. Then I started thinking that I should call the local blood bank to make a donation. *Maybe*, I thought, *I should even eat some cookies to keep my strength up!*

I was feeling woozy as the pain of one cut was added to the burning of the next gash. I shaved the second leg as fast as I could, which, as seasoned shavers know, is usually a bad idea. I'm not sure if I was more anxious about leaving DNA evidence and Mom being mad that I messed up the bathroom or about the possibility of me leaving a corpse behind. In a panic, I taped a ring of mini pads around my ankle to absorb the platelets that gravity had led on a swift escape mission. I remembered that my dad put dabs of toilet paper on his cuts after shaving. So I placed tiny tourniquets on all the puncture wounds but the blood soaked through quickly and I had to keep replacing the blobs of paper. My legs resembled a vandalized middle-school bathroom ceiling.

Rinsing the second leg, bent up under my chin in the sink, the water made the open abrasions sting. I remembered from a first-aid class that I needed to Stop! Drop! And Roll! No, wait, that's not it. I needed to apply pressure to stop the bleeding. Of course I didn't dare stain one of Mom's good towels so I wrapped Frankenstein gauze to firmly press against the dozens of clumps of soggy tissue scattered around my lower extremities. Eventually most of the bleeding clotted under the snagged skin patches, or at least slowed to a manageable trickle. Feeling really faint by now, I covered my many wounds with bandages. Then I cleaned up the horror scene. I discreetly hid all the red plasma-covered paper and pads in the wastebasket and scrubbed a few lingering drops of evidence out of the rug. As nonchalantly as possible I exited the bathroom and headed down the hall with skinned knees, slit ankles and gashed shins. I hoped I wouldn't run into anyone who would expect an explanation. They'd probably think it was some radical but failed suicide attempt.

As it turned out my dad came home at that moment and looked up the staircase at me. He laughed, and then escorted me back to the slaughter room. He introduced me to various methods and products to stop bleeding. One of them was a salt-like substance that caused pulsating pain. I panted and blew to handle the discomfort. (In later years I realized it was a great training for the Lamaze technique.) Dad snickered the whole way through my initiation as he administered salt to my wounds and watched me squirm. (I always feared he might use that same method on me again during my rebellious teen years.) I would learn to become a better shaver in time so I wouldn't have to use that dreadful stuff again. But I still bear some scars as a reminder of the experience.

Over the years I have tried many alternate methods for getting rid of unwanted hair. I have used the "revolutionary" device that literally tears the hairs out of your legs by the roots. The first step in the process involved hiding in pants for weeks in the middle of summer, while I grew my leg hair out like fur. (I could have just braided them and been done with it.) Every time I left the house I prayed I wouldn't get into an accident. Then I'd have to explain to some gorgeous paramedic about my science experiment. Or, worse yet, end up in the morgue on that famous cable show that features the puzzled coroner doing her final exam. The camera would close in on my hairy legs and the nametag around my toe, and then pan back to her confused raised-eyebrow look. My worst nightmare!

Finally my leg hair was long enough. Locked up in the privacy of my own torture chamber (back to the bathroom again), I sweated profusely as I tried to yank the coarse hair (which no doubt made it extra difficult) out of my pores. The sensation of the multiple pain pricks made my nerves jitter. Who could have thought of such a pastime, I wonder? It ranks up there with some of the most excruciatingly painful experiences of my life. I learned after many attempts that I couldn't do it without at least three beers to relax me first. And the promise of a well-deserved chocolate reward afterwards. It took me longer to mow my legs than it did to mow the lawn. My legs would become blotchy and red which took hours to recover from and also for the seizure-like twitching to subside. As for doing my bikini line, the manufacturer is absolutely crazy. No one is going anywhere near there! I'd have to be sedated first. This device could be a prison reform system, for Pete's sake. If you commit a crime you could receive a sentence of THROB. Total Hair Removal On Body! I'm telling you, that surely would deter repeat offenders.

Then some brilliant mind came up with hot wax hair removal. For me, this is another form of self-induced craziness. I actually gave it a try too, once. I was locked in my bathroom (a woman's name for a workshop), thinking I was doing myself a grand favor by waxing my legs. I was hoping they would become supple, smooth and sexy, just like in the commercials. With my leg propped up on the counter, I spread the hot wax on my legs with a plastic spatula. The honey-like substance was indeed very hot and immediately adhered to my skin like Super-Glue. I opened the window to cool the hot wax and my perspiration. I began placing the tape strips onto the sticky residue, leaving a small piece to grip at one end.

I couldn't help but ponder for a moment why we didn't follow the Europeans' lead, and just where did our hair-removal obsession come from? It is such a nuisance! I mean, really…a little stubble does help to keep my pantyhose from slipping. I wish we would have left well enough alone. If men don't feel like shaving, they just call it "hunting season." When is our hunting season, I'd like to know?

Confident that having smooth legs would be so worth it, I yanked a strip. Ouch! I pulled again. *Oh my God, oh my God*, I started to chant. As I pulled, my skin lifted away from my body. That's when I realized I had to be quick, like I was removing a Band-Aid. Relying on my high pain tolerance, I yanked the tape again. Holy crap! The stuff was not coming off! Beads of sweat popped out onto my upper lip and my heart began to pound.

I thought I'd just scrape the spackle off slowly by tugging on a corner and lifting it up. It wouldn't budge. I frantically tried to reheat the wax with the blow dryer and by running it under hot water, hoping it would soften. Frightened that I might be stuck that way forever, I realized there was no turning back. I was going to have to rip the stuff off of me like I was skinning a deer. Mentally I encouraged myself as I prepared to grab on and thrust with all my might. *If thousands of other women can do it, I sure should be able to do it too!* I preached to myself. But thinking all along, *There has got to be a better way!* Yikes!

I have a friend who has the time and patience to have electrolysis performed on her legs. Every square inch! Week after week, she goes for one hour to endure the tedious task of having the hairs removed one by one by one. Each visit they smooth out another square area, leaving her with checkerboard legs. (Incidentally, she plays one hell of a game of chess.) I admire her perseverance in attacking each little devil standing erect whose mere purpose is humiliation, but I'm more of a short-term goal person myself. I look for a more immediate solution that is a bit more private.

Each one of these violent methods was horrifying to me but I can't imagine how it has become a group sport. There is nothing appealing to me about bearing my embarrassing follicle-filled legs (among other body parts) to a stranger at a boutique. And paying to induce that kind of torture upon me while trying to be brave, hiding my contorted facial expressions and smothering screeching outcries—I don't think so! More power to those ladies who can do it, but I think that if you are really that starved for social activity, I'd suggest a Tupperware party.

I have also tried depilatory creams and lotions. Their ingredients were strong enough to curl my toes and peel the wallpaper off my walls, but wouldn't you know my coarse gorilla stubble was left behind. Lastly, some women find satisfaction in laser hair removal. Quite honestly I'm a little reluctant to try it ever since I saw a light saber take off a limb in *Star Wars*. How can light be that powerful? I might consider it if they could shave off a couple inches of extra weight, though.

I seem to be most compatible with old-fashioned shaving. I have actually gotten pretty good at it as a veteran shaver. There is one area that is tough to work around and these bony knees are what keep the challenge alive. On occasion I nick myself when I get a little too confident. I have even become so skilled I can shave while I drive but only in a pinch.

I recently was involved in a car accident caused by someone else. Afterward they took me to the emergency room to be examined. The handsome doctor gave me anesthesia to repair my various wounds, and then remarked that nothing seemed to be life-threatening and I would recover just fine.

Then he added: "How did you get that strip of wax on your leg?"

"Oh, it's a science experiment I've been working on for quite some time," I replied with a beet-red face.

I swiftly rolled my pant legs back down and asked to be discharged right away as my ride was waiting. This was my opportunity to get home quickly and yank the lingering wax off of me while I was still very heavily sedated and would feel no pain. Choose your method carefully, ladies!

As hair-raising as that was, wait until you see what the next phase brings!

CHAPTER 3

What Came First, The Chicken or The Egg?

It was a long-awaited spring-like day in late April. The sun rose high and its intense rays warmed the air that swirled around my body. Carefree and childlike, I sped down the block to my friend Kathy's house. The wheels on my skates thumped as I passed over each crack in the sidewalk. I stretched out my arms like a tightrope artist, attempting to keep my balance as my feet struggled awkwardly to stay underneath me.

Breaking my concentration for a moment, I looked up at Kathy who was shooting some hoops in front of her garage. Suddenly I was conscious of a nauseated sensation and a cramp in my lower abdomen, and was happy to reach my destination. Turning the corner onto her driveway, the toe of my skate caught on a low spot and I took a tumble to the ground. I lay there wiping myself off and assessing my scraped forearms and other injuries spotted with blood and loose gravel. Pain stretched across my jarred pelvis. All at once it seemed hilarious and we roared with laughter. Then Kathy laced up her skates and we coasted back down her drive adorned in our stylish wheels. Clumsily we giggled our way back to my house. Oh, what simple, un-complicated pre-teen lives we had.

My breathing was labored and my stomach ached upon arrival. I went in the house to rest a minute and to change out of my torn pants. Lo and behold, my jeans were all bloodied on the inside. *Oh my gosh, I'm bleeding internally!* I thought. It must have been quite a traumatic fall. Alarmed and confused, I summoned my mother for advice. Ohhh! Then it all became clearer. Surprise! So that's what that fifth-grade filmstrip was about!

My mother gave me a warm, gushing welcome-to-woman-hood hug and handed me an elastic belt and a feminine pad that was as big as the banana seat on my bike, minus the aerodynamics. I might as well have put an announcement tattoo on my forehead. There was no way I could successfully smuggle (and conceal) the padded life-preserver belt, into my hip hugger pants. The massive thing went from my navel around to the tip of my butt crease. My greatest fear was that if the damn thing got completely saturated, the weight of it would take me down in an instant. Running through sprinklers, swimming, getting caught in the rain or having an ice bucket jubilantly dumped on me after a victorious win could prove to be devastating. It's hard to keep your legs together like a lady when there's a bloating saddle between them like a toddler's saggy diaper.

I wasn't very excited about this new phase in my life. Unexpectedly finding a gory, bloody scene inside my own britches was really kind of a dirty trick to play on a young, unsuspecting girl who was happily minding her own business. Sometimes these "periods" were accompanied by warning signs such as two days of bloating like a puffer-fish, tender breasts swelling and a nauseous crampy feeling like having a roll of fat accidentally caught in my zipper. Other months there were no warnings whatsoever. Just a mess caused from an overachieving ovary whose job was to expel an egg whether filling a request or not.

Quite frankly, at that point I didn't get what all the excitement was about and really wasn't sure if I wanted to be a woman yet! The whole concept seemed pretty complicated and I felt a little chicken having to deliver the egg. Boys weren't terribly impressive to me and the thought of all the commotion about fallopian tubes and fertilization appeared to be far more of a benefit for them, than for us girls. How typical is that? I wondered why I couldn't just be left alone to go on roller-skating for awhile.

I had barely outgrown and packed away my naked Barbies and was still preoccupied with pogo sticks and hula hoops for goodness sake! My Raggedy Ann doll could still be found stuffed between my mattress and wall and most likely was missing a shoe. Her braided hair, dangling down, was mingling with the dust bunnies under my bed. I had a pet dog that I would feed only when he would sit next to his empty dish and beg for me to fill it. The most significant mothering experience on my résumé to date was keeping a fish alive for eight days.

I was barely responsible enough to take care of my own pierced ears without my mother having to assist me with those bleeding holes. Admittedly, my lack of care caused many infections. It is almost inconceivable (pun intended) to think that at that young age I was physiologically prepared to conceive and harbor a child and yet my parents didn't think I was old enough to ride my bike to the opposite end of town.

I usually avoided yuk at all cost. Like the time I had to watch the neighbor kid until his mother got home. His diaper was loaded with toxic waste and smelled atrocious. I claimed I didn't smell a thing as I collected my pay and hurried home.

I hadn't even mastered drinking milk and laughing at the same time without it coming out my nose. I constantly forgot where I left my diary key and felt squeamish when I saw blood surrounding a loose tooth. Yikes! How could my almighty mastermind have thought I was mature enough to be the guardian of a glorious hemorrhaging womb?

And why in heaven's name is it called a "period" anyway? If it consisted of one sole drop of blood, like the small blotch you get on a Band-Aid after drawing blood, that would be conceivable. But when the ritual lasts for many weary days on end and we poor anemic girls have to ingest iron supplements and nearly need a blood transfusion, I think it is at the very least deserving of a title such as "semi-colon" or, better yet, "exclamation point." The term "period" is too miniscule and just doesn't seem to do it justice.

Leave it to women to be so prepared and equipped for life that from the date of our birth, our ovaries are loaded and ready to release eggs at timed intervals like a pitching machine in a batting cage. Yet there is a certain unpredictability (kind of like a galactic shootout) that adds to their feminine indecisiveness. If only we could order up what we want: scrambled, fried, over easy or sunny side up. Instead the greater challenge is to figure out their release date based on if we want to produce egglets or not. Unfortunately it is usually when we are trying to avoid offspring that our eggs are the most seductively confrontational. And the hostess, who is trying to conceive, seems to have eggs with hardened shells and elusive powers.

Unfortunately, every month we are faced with the challenge of finding the best way to deal with our ovulation clearance. Over the years, feminine hygiene products have made remarkable advances. Just put a plug in and go—the tampon is an innovative classic. The maxi pad went from bleacher seat cushions down to micro mini pads the size of a computer chip with the miraculous absorbency of day-old sponge cake. Some have wings, although their adhesion is intended to stick to our undergarments, so the pad won't fly away. But occasionally they develop their own agenda and try to walk down the inside of my pant leg like a starfish searching for new territory, which is a real impediment to my gait. When this happens I'm forced to inconspicuously stretch and shake my leg. It seems to be the only way while in public to get its tentacles to release and reattach itself to my panty.

We women spend much of our lives literally going in circles.

We are either pre, present or post menstrual cycle. We are always trying to plan in, on or around its cyclical path. We anticipate its arrival and plan honeymoons, triathlons, swimwear modeling and gynecological visits around it. When we are maternally turned on, we are trying to reproduce using premeditated, timely seduction and are quite disappointed at the first sign of plasma and must wait for thirty days to try again. At other times we are avoiding sexual stimuli during free-radical ovulation. Occasionally there is a terrifying delay and tremendous relief when bloodshed appears. Then there's the calm before the storm, which is the restful state prior to coming full circle, and beginning it all over again.

We spend by far more vicious cycles trying to shun the ovum than pursue it. Some women count days on a calendar and take their daily temperature to get in sync with their bodies' normal rhythm. Some eggs are guarded by abstinence and chastity belts. Other girls use foams, rubber sheaths and strategically placed instruments to repel any reproductive cells that may have slipped past the inattentive gatekeeper to the birthing chamber. Many females consume pills, place patches or get shots to evaporate any hormonal upheaval, to avoid having a cycle at all, as a prevention which in turn saves the life of the once-executed rabbit. Some ladies just pray, **a lot!**

These days there are so many options that one can easily get confused. Once I greeted my husband with a bottle of wine, the exciting news that I got an IUD and the sexy promise that I would take him for the carefree ride of his life. He angrily grabbed the glass of wine out of my hand and took away my car keys. "I said I got an IUD," I blurted, "not a DUI!"

Whatever the method, it is the woman who is most actively involved in making the decisions that affect her own body and future. We are educating ourselves and have overcome being naïve and waiting until the honeymoon to ask in a startled tone, "You're going to put what, *where?*"

Female sexuality has changed immensely throughout history. Women have decided that if we are the ones manufacturing and in charge of logistical management of this commodity, we want to have more say about the who, what, where, when, how and why of the fertilization process. Why should we not get to have some fun with it all? And if we have anything to say about it, the future will reach orgasmic new heights. In fact I know many ladies who share the mentality that if you want something done right, you've got to do it yourself.

Our automated bodies usually prove to be miraculous well-oiled machines that just keep reliably producing, regardless of supply or demand. We were entrusted with the splendid gift and responsibility of life-generating genes well before we knew how to use them or even cared. We are able to expand our family tree, fuller than any other in the orchard if we choose. We are also capable of becoming fertilized far beyond what I think is our mentally or physically able age. Getting pregnant in your late forties could be the ultimate dirty trick.

Our years of service begin with a "period" and end with many question marks. Why was I given 442 eggs when I only needed four? Amazingly, my body knew to pick out the best ones too! Some women, for various reasons, forgo the birthing process. I think they should be given a free pass out of the whole dramatic uterine cleansing and hot flash routine.

Considering the splendid magnitude of the event when conception is achieved, I believe it's shameful how little recognition women receive for the long, uncomfortable months to bring forth and hatch the perfect egg. They are deserving of gifts and extreme gratitude from their mate. By gosh there is more hoopla with bells and sirens when someone wins $116 at a casino from the fifty-cent slot machines than there is at the fragile moment of conception. Why all the mystery, mental preparation and dipsticks? Couldn't there be a bell that rings when we hit the jackpot?

And talk about an unsuspecting girl minding her own business. Imagine Mary roller-skating along one day with her glorious womb, when she was blinded by the Immaculate Conception of her overachieving ovary. She probably remarked in a justifiably stunned tone, "Ah, so that's what those fifth-grade hieroglyphics were about! You're going to put what, *where*?" Poor thing was shocked; she wasn't even aware that she had been having her exclamation point or should have been guarding the gate! It can be wondrous being thrust into womanhood, and complicating to say the least, but at least Mary got some angels to appear for her grand hoopla surprise! The rest of us search for precise recollection of our actions (most of them not so pure), check dates on the calendar and are forced to wait patiently for the first sign of splendid swelling and queasiness!

In my case it sure sounds like the chicken came first!

CHAPTER 4
Weight of Gold

My big bones were a curse from birth. I'm sure I was bigger than a size four when I was a toddler; so dress sizes have always been difficult for me to comprehend and I surely don't get how "0" can equal a size. Could one even feel proud about being a "0"? (Maybe I'm just jealous.) I do believe that beauty is only skin deep and inner beauty is what really matters and should count. But in today's warped society, "thin is in" is the message that subconsciously bombards girls beginning at a very young age and continues to haunt most of us, all our lives. Somewhere between the stage when I would jump out of my diaper and streak through the house filled with company, free from inhibitions, to the age when I would try on my older (yet smaller) sister's hand-me-downs that I had already outgrown, my it's-okay-to-be-me philosophy was shattered.

A perception which I can't seem to escape comes from the old fairy tale about the Bear family. The images of a big, tall, masculine Papa Bear, a medium-sized Mama Bear and a wee little Baby Bear are stuck in my head. I realize it isn't realistic that we all fit the diagram, nor healthy to be type-cast in that mold. However, no matter if they are stick people, cartoons or animals, the characters in my head all seem to have the same proportions.

My self-image was similar to a distorted circus mirror—I appeared squatty and short with chubby limbs. Then I had a growth spurt that caused an alteration. Before the opportunity was lost I wanted to take advantage of the metabolism frenzy. I finally had a figure worthy of a bikini and the confidence to wear one in public the summer prior to my freshman year of high-school.

My mom took me shopping to find just the right suit that would accentuate the positive. I put on my new suit and headed over to my friend Jenny's house where we were gathering to go to the beach. Petite little Jenny came out of her room wearing exactly the same swimsuit. I was horrified. What were the chances of that happening? Yes, I did have a bigger bust line but it was still no match for a great-looking little butt, thin long legs and flat tummy you could bounce a quarter off of. What an ego buster that was!

The image of Daddy's Little Girl really exploded when I became pregnant. In fact, people started to sarcastically call me "Tiny." I was catapulted into the big Papa Bear size category. I had an insatiable appetite and could put just about any man to shame bellying up to a buffet. Finally being able to eat for two (adults, that is) without the guilt—I loved being pregnant. I was so excited to be showing, I pushed my tummy out until my navel protruded and popped. The most shocking thing of all was when I weighed in just prior to delivery; I tipped the scale to a greater weight than Papa Bear himself!

Let's face it. I've been hiding and disguising my body for years. I keep my back and butt to the wall if at all possible. During the times in my life when it was inevitable that my rear end had to face a crowd, thank goodness it was hidden under a billowing commencement gown with padded shoulders or a bridal dress with multiple layers of silk, French lace and draping beads which led the eye away. I wore high heels whenever possible—for that elongated appearance. But just how high do my stilts need to be to make my height look proportionate to weight?

Weight Watchers. What a funny concept. I've spent most of my life avoiding standing still long enough so that no one would have an opportunity to get a good look at my weight. I sure didn't want to bring attention to myself and certainly not ask others to watch. Weighing myself on the scale in front of others is a ghastly notion. I'd be more likely to agree to it if they were liquored up and willing to stick dollar bills in my straps.

Years ago a friend begged me to go with her to a support meeting because that is what we friends do for one another. It was held in a church basement, alongside the Optimists Club. In fact, I think the dues are 50% off if you join both at the same time. They do seem to go hand in hand. It seems like most members are confident hopefuls professing their dreams of good fortune, good deeds and weight loss to gain contentment.

I'd rather have socialized with my friend at a custard shop with a waffle cone, but if it was my moral support that she needed, I'd be there. We circled the parking lot looking for any recognizable vehicles, and then parked inconspicuously. She explained that the week prior she saw a teacher that she knew so she ducked into the pet supply store next door and ended up buying a twenty-pound bag of kibbles. She doesn't even own a dog.

"It's only seventeen miles to the next town," I suggested. "We don't know anyone there. We could stop at my house and pick up a wig and funny glasses." She rolled her eyes at me.

One thing I can tell you for sure, the meeting was not a spectator sport. I, Inspector Gadget with my collar up and dark sunglasses on, along with my friend (who shall remain nameless to protect the innocent) sat in the back row to observe. We watched one lady stripping all but her soul for her initial weigh-in. She removed her press-on fingernails, false eyelashes, wedding band, and every stitch of clothing except her antique-white undies and Band-Aids for a bra. I can only guess she had been fasting since the Tuesday before. Then she stalled, swishing her hair back and forth to evaporate the final heavy moisture from the shower she took earlier. Maybe she needed the support of the crowd to cheer her on.

Now correct me if I'm wrong, but if it were my turn to weigh in, I'd have loaded up my trench coat with bricks and worn wool socks, pewter bracelets and two layers of foundation cream. My pockets would be full of change and I'd throw in an extra IUD for good measure. After an evening of drinking heavy dark beer and eating fondue and cheesecake, I'd saunter up to the scale in waders. You know exactly where I'm going with this, don't you? That way it would increase the odds of losing twenty-pounds to hit my goal weight. I'm optimistically all about happy endings. I'd just prefer to be alone, without a crowd of onlookers. To each his own!

In the privacy of my own home I tried ordering calorie-controlled meals through the mail as another method of weight loss. Never was I quite as ravenous as when I had to wait, nose to glass, for the UPS driver to approach my house with my long-awaited balanced portions of nutrition. I nearly took a bite out of him (making him the sixth food group) when he stuck his arm in my door. It was a similar starvation to when the doctor instructed me to fast for twelve hours before having blood work done. Just the suggestion of having to wait to eat, spirals me into an obsessive sense of famine.

There was the infamous Atkins diet. Boy, it worked wonders! But for me it was quite a transformation of my eating habits. I'm not usually carnivorous, but meat was on the menu for breakfast, lunch and dinner. My favorite food became whipped cream in the can. It had less than one carbohydrate. Anything that had the < symbol in front of the number one was equivalent to free intake. I could mentally justify eating a wheelbarrow of whipped cream because it was basically a zero carb intake. It was fabulous right out of the can and especially on top of a cold brat or pork chop for breakfast. I wore a holster to sport my dispenser so that I'd be sure to meet my quota of dairy intake disguised as sweet aerosol-induced fluff.

One time I visited Los Angeles, the purposefully thin capital of the world. When I got off the plane, Security nabbed me in front of a crowd. It was so humiliating. The dogs sniffed out my luggage. The guards tore open my suitcase and confiscated an ounce of cocoa, my jumbo-sized Snickers bars and my prescription bottles filled with M&M's. They insisted that upon my return I better have a doctor's affidavit and X-rays to prove I am indeed big-boned or I'd be escorted to the nearest health spa. Don't you think we have become a little overly obsessed?

I'll admit my desire for candy and chocolate was not always a problem. But the older I get the stronger it has become. Or maybe I'm more willing to admit that the suppressed urges are real and act on them. Similar to sex but even more orgasmic! It's amazing what I would do for a few Double Stuffed Oreos or Fudge Nut Dream Bars. And after being introduced to peanut butter sauce I knew I had a problem. You can smear it on anything (even Brussels sprouts) and it tastes great. There is a drug called Ecstasy. In my fantasy world my idea of euphoric Ecstasy would be sucking down a Double Death Chocolate Swirl cake slathered with peanut butter sauce and whipped cream on top alongside a scoop of softened ice cream. Satisfying my ridiculous cravings and my munchies all in one. Wow, man! Dinner was great.

I guess you could call me a chocoholic. There, I said it! No more hiding Hershey's Kisses in my shoes or lying about carrot cake being good for my eye condition. It became apparent that I had a problem when I found myself in the closet one day with a bag of Reese's Peanut Butter Cups that was meant for a first-grade class treat. They were each supposed to get two and I uncontrollably ate so many that each child ended up with a half of one wrapped in plastic wrap and I concocted a story about a raccoon getting into the bag.

Ice cream is another weakness. I used to rush out when I heard the music of the ice cream truck coming and chase it down the street, passing up the small children to get my novelties. I've become much more sophisticated over the years. Now I have my very own "dealer." My Schwan's man is a good-looking hunk who delivers forty-one flavors of delectable frozen aphrodisiac right to my door, any day of the week I like. Yum! He thinks I run a daycare. Little does he know I'm just a suppressed homemaker trying to fulfill my desires with sinful and palatable rewards.

But with indulgences comes signs of consequences. Not even "cellulite" is a polite word for fat. It is a sign of trouble when we start to give cute names like "love handles" and "speed bumps" to our rolls and saddle-bags. When the lowest setting of dimming the lights is no longer sufficient and lying flat is no longer attainable, it is time to acknowledge the need for change. I'll let Kris, my lover-boy, wear the sexy lingerie.

Exercise might be the only solution to support my habit. I try to ride five miles per day on my stationary bike. I can even multi-task and average folding about a load of laundry per mile. After about two loads or a couple of miles I turn the bike around to face the other direction for a change of scenery while killing two less-than fun tasks at one time.

Some clothing fads are truly the fashion industry's way of pulling a cruel prank on all of us. The eye of the beholder must be able to look honestly in the mirror at our own image and concede that "they" (whoever "they" are) aren't really designing the current style for the vast population but merely for the 10% who comprise the fashion skinny club. Quite frankly, most women should not be sporting bare midriffs, muffin tops, whale tails or plumber's cracks (you are exempt of course, if you are one).

Also, not all of us are meant to embrace thong underwear. It's hard to hide behind strings. And growing up, one of our main missions in life was to keep anything and everything from sliding into that crack. Now, intentionally placing something in there in the name of fashion can be both liberating and trendy. You'll feel like you're getting away with something huge. Go for it, girly!

Psychologists have concurred that it can be unhealthy to use food as a reward. Well, my theory is all about balance and moderation. If I can rationalize that it takes about 6 ½ mini candy bars to equal one full-size bar, and a diet soda reduces the total sum to approximately 4 ½, then a bike ride absolves 2 ½, leaving me with two little candy bars for my indulgence; I so deserve it! I say the guilt of eating them in the closet will ruin their taste altogether, and guilt is by far unhealthier.

So bring your goodie bag out of the closet and face the green grass. When you are overweight all you see are thin people. When you are thin all you see are Dairy Queen signs. Most of us have ridden the ups and downs, and need to find the happy medium and the method that works best to keep us there, instead of trying to fool everyone by dieting every five years prior to our class reunion to prove we didn't let ourselves go. Maybe letting go and being real should be the attitude that secures the "Most Likely to Succeed" award. Or just write on your nametag, *I'm not fat, I'm pregnant!* That'll surely give them something else to talk about.

There's no doubt about it, being grossly overweight can cause a myriad of health problems. You know you're too heavy when a liposuction procedure will take more than one visit. It is also obvious that being the best you can be is a great boost for anyone's self-esteem, and that is what we should all strive for. It's time to embrace the "it's okay to be me" attitude!

Men produce their best results by the suggestion and promise of a sexual reward. I myself can be most productive with the promise of a tantalizing morsel of dessert. Who knows, if my mate puts on a sexy thong, and feeds me a cupcake I might just dole out a sexual treat for a change instead of having a headache. See how well this works for everyone?

And talk about a double standard. Men seem to be most unfairly obsessed with women's bodies and tend to scrutinize the imperfections of the female form on a regular basis. Yet I know just as many overweight males that have no desire to improve their image or better themselves for the likes of us girls. At least I lost most of the baby weight. Some guys look like they are stuck in their third trimester, including the man boobs!

I lost a few pounds and decided I'm going to embrace the real me. I'm planning another trip to Los Angeles as an ego booster. This time I'm bringing proof, so airport security picks on someone their own size!

See Following Affidavit:

My patient
Bonnie Lowell

has been examined by myself and I find her to be in fact very big-boned.

Her bone age has the maturity of 2 ½ years beyond her current age.

SIGNED:

Bernard Huizenga M.D.

CHAPTER 5
Natural Childbirth?

As I've divulged in a previous chapter, I was not particularly smitten by boys as a teen. I could hardly be aroused by their gross gestures or immature male bonding rituals. As far as I was concerned, there wasn't enough Musk cologne to disguise the strange array of acne cream, axle grease and rotten foot odors that permeated their cool exteriors. And they generally created a lot of dirt. Clutter seemed to follow them everywhere. I don't have a problem with getting dirty; in my opinion it just shouldn't be a lifestyle!

Now there were exceptions to the rule, mind you. There *were* male specimens that turned my head occasionally, but once I had to rule out blood relatives, my eighth-grade drama teacher and my doctor as possible dating pool material, there weren't many left that tickled my fancy in the slightest way. I just knew for sure that I wanted to have kids. Lots of them! But early on I was pretty clueless about how I would achieve that. I knew we needed men for some reason but I just wasn't really getting the concept! Was I the bird? The bee? Should I mate with another bird or cross-pollinate with a bee? Does anyone know who started these rumors and if there is any validity to it? Or is that part of the mystery—getting stung a few times just trying to figure it all out?

I know my mother must have felt she did an adequate job explaining the birds and the bees and who plays what role. I'm sure she covered the love and marriage parts but quite frankly the true meaning was lost in translation. Because frightening to admit, all I heard was, "When two people are, *together* and close for awhile….." For goodness sake! Is it a wonder why, being equipped with merely those lame instructions, I never would sit still again? I was afraid to rub up against anyone for too long. I needed more information. How close? How long is awhile? Can I kick him out of the nest or sting him if I do not like it?

Thank goodness for my mature and knowledgeable friend Debbie who finally answered all of my inquiries when I was certainly old enough to know better but was shocked none-the-less when she divulged the gory reproductive details. *No! That's nasty, Debbie. Are you sure? Eeyou!!*

Well, years later, the whole sex craze continued to be a mystery but out of respect for my husband I polished my acting skills to follow the trend. I could have achieved more orgasmic pleasure by making love to a piece of cheesecake myself. But as long as there was a combination of good kissing, an active imagination and, yes, a piece of turtle cheesecake on the nightstand to entice me….. I knew babies would come.

Each month my flirtatious and anxious eggs were on the prowl to find their mate. My unsuspecting husband's sexual weakness would succumb to my irresistible advances. His dazed and amorous sperm searched the dark cavern for an abrupt, less than romantic interchange similar to the frenzy of desperate males at bar time, looking for a mate.

Sure enough! After a few ambitious and persevering months of temptress seduction the fruits of my labor took hold. I was a shoo-in for an Academy Award. The seeds had been sown; the fertilization fiesta was a success and my little zygote afforded me a new identity that would change my life forever. I was finally a baby mama to a miniscule embryo!

I was ecstatic to be pregnant and how fitting to find it out on the day of New Year's Eve! I planned out the itinerary for every last cigarette (knowing I needed to quit right away) to last me until the stroke of midnight. I hovered around a communal ashtray, bonding with a small group of optimistic yet desperate quitters. We leaned in and passed around our final cigarette, puffing away, as the seconds counted down.

A worn smudge mark formed on each date on the calendar from counting and recalculating 280 days until the suspenseful delivery date. Depending on whether conception occurred after my late-night bowling celebration on Thursday from a 220 score…or maybe it was during the brief 34-minute romantic interlude between my cousin's wedding and reception the following Saturday. Then again the magical moment could have been on the Monday a week prior when my husband received a passionate thank-you in the pantry for helping me get a can of string beans off the upper shelf I couldn't reach myself. Regardless, the new focus in our existence would be the upcoming "due" date.

I had to swallow pre-natal vitamins larger than the fetus itself until its second trimester. I got nauseous at the smell of beef cooking and yet with my ravenous appetite I could challenge any man to eat a side of beef at a buffet table. I just had to tolerate the sizzling taste of Tabasco sauce heart-burn in the back of my throat as an unwanted result.

Hurray! No more holding my tummy in. I could finally exhale and relax my stomach muscles. My body bloated like a Cabbage Patch doll. My ankles swelled so much they equaled the diameter of my thighs. They were like elephant legs. I could press an indentation into the water-gorged swollen skin that would stay pitted for hours. If ever I was short of pencil and paper I could etch notes or reminder phone numbers into my ankles for cripe sake!

Pregnancy is a tremendous way to get in touch with your body. For some reason everyone else thinks they can touch your body as well. Acquaintances rubbed my Buddha belly as if hoping I would grant them three wishes. One of my co-workers continually gave me an update every time he saw me: "Mama, you gettin' round!" My girlish figure dissolved; as the sides of my hourglass shape ballooned, my focus on time consumed me. And my once-inverted navel protruded like a marble, popping out just like a thermometer in a cooked turkey screaming "I'm plump and done!"

With pregnancy comes some abstinence. No hot tubs, amusement park rides, martinis, aerobics, kitty litter boxes, tobacco products, crash diets, sit-ups, strenuous snow shoveling or exposure to deadly fumes from cleaning products. One day I even had to tough my way through the removal of an impacted wisdom tooth with little pain medication so as not to harm my baby. It was another way to test my Lamaze breathing. (Somehow I doubt women really forget how to breathe in the delivery room.)

Speaking of Lamaze—my strong-willed, can-do attitude took me to a birthing class in a church basement one evening. I was surrounded by fellow mothers filled with excitement and anticipation of a natural childbirth experience. We bonded as we all soaked up as much education about the process as possible. At the onset of the meeting we chatted together, comparing details about our Kegel exercises, hemorrhoids and morning sickness, as bowls of snacks balanced on our bellies. We watched a shocking filmstrip depicting a weary woman in excruciating pain, her ankles spread as wide as the Grand Canyon, the hospital crew gazing inside her gaping opening, tugging and prying at it to gain access to the hidden treasure. When it was over we all left, starkly pale, quiet and stunned. Our confidence was shattered. Reality struck that there was no turning back! Childbirth seemed to be the only way to get that baby out of our bodies. I incoherently murmured in disbelief as we climbed the stairs, "I don't think I can do that!"

Natural childbirth? Natural is when your eyes squint at the sun or to peek while kissing. Natural is asking someone to smell something, to verify that it smells horrible. Natural is licking oozing frosting off the wrapper from your donut or the three-second rule of blowing the dirt off of food when it falls on the floor. Natural is running your gas gauge all the way down to E or feeling cunning while speeding past a parked squad car and noticing that the patrolperson is too preoccupied by the ketchup stain on their uniform to notice.

But *natural childbirth??* There is nothing natural about a group of strangers viewing parts of my body that are so private even I have never seen them before. My mother and I had previously worked pretty hard to keep my privates under wraps. Thus my self-conscious, squeamish reaction that had me feeling faint at the thought of my personal vaginal cavity becoming the teaching tool for new staff interns or the leading role in a feature film for PBS.

So when I finally arrived at the hospital, I found out quickly it wasn't the place to get special or speedy treatment when you're having a baby. They've seen it plenty of times before, therefore it's nothing to get excited about. The admittance clerk will sit by and wait through as many contractions as it takes for you to produce an insurance card and verify your mother's maiden name. At the elevators the food carts got first priority and the nurses sprang from their station to aid some guy whining about passing a couple of tiny gallstones. Boo hoo!

Once in my assigned birthing room a nurse resembling a cranky Mother Teresa insisted that the dribble running down my leg was probably my bladder leaking. I was a grown woman who was nine and a half months' pregnant and had been in labor for twelve hours by that time. I think I knew the difference between my bag of water leaking or if I was peeing in my pants for God's sake!

Soon after that, my doctor dropped in to tell me I looked like I was having too much fun to be in *hard* labor so he wanted me up, walking the halls. Great. It felt like I had a watermelon sagging in my fanny pack. I was weak in the knees and couldn't straighten upright anymore but sure, I thought to myself, I'd love to go for a walk with my butt hanging out the back of my gown and leaving a dribble of amniotic fluid (I mean pee) down the hallway. Men! I'm surprised he didn't suggest I help hand out breakfast trays while I was up!

When the time came all modesty was lost. My subconscious mind succumbed to the process of strangers literally getting into my business. I became delirious as the pain consumed me. It was like a blood pressure tourniquet was squeezing and tightening around my whole body with each contraction. The staff's faces began to blend together as my preoccupation with cleansing breaths and He He He Hah overwhelmed me. Any previous self-consciousness disappeared nor did I now really care who looked under my gown. The lady from the cafeteria came in to see if I wanted Jell-O and I think she even looked underneath to see if the baby's head was crowning. Oh well, the more the merrier!

After many continuous hard hours of working with rebellious contractions I tried desperately to hang onto my optimism and "if millions of other women have done this I can do it too" attitude. With my legs flailing wide open I called out, "Somebody come check me!" A male nurse leaned in. "You've got a long way to go," he said, shaking his head. He crushed almost all of the spirit I had left. That face I remember! His image is embedded in my brain and if I ever run into that guy again we'll see if my size seven and a half shoe up his rear end is more or less equivalent to an eight and a half pound baby coming out of my bottom.

Anxious and ready now that the moment of unveiling was finally upon us and that I had skirted my near-death experience, my body instinctively went into an incredible insatiable urge to push. I looked to my husband and partner for guidance and support as I shared the news. His brilliant advice was to cross my legs. "Cross my legs," I repeated in an *are-you-crazy?* tone. "I will not! I came here to have a baby by gosh and that's what I'm going to do!"

I had been patient up until then with him shoving ice chips into my mouth whether I wanted them or not. I'd kept my cool when he commented, "That wasn't such a bad one," assessing the jumping needle on the monitor showing contraction strength as my nostrils flared and knuckles whitened. I had tolerated laboring mothers who'd come in after me, ignoring their screams as they passed down the halls, celebrating with them as they were delivering and now wheeled past me, with their bundles of joy swaddled in their arms, while I was still panting and blowing!—It was finally my turn, damn it! "Call the nurse," I said to my husband. He stood there dumbfounded. So I summoned my own nurse like I was hailing a cab.

Wanting to put an end to the horrendous pain I pushed so hard my ears popped. The mucus plug in my cervix exploded. Blood vessels in my neck bulged as my face turned flare-red. My remaining bag of water burst, causing white-water rapids to gush down the slanted table. It ricocheted and splashed upon the nurse who had just peered in to check for full dilation. Her glasses became spotted with fluid and her look of disgust at her sopping scrub uniform told me her hourly rate wasn't an adequate exchange. Momentarily I felt guilty while she questioned her career choice. *That's what she gets for sticking her head in there so close,* I thought, but I didn't say anything.

She distracted us both by placing a big round mirror at the foot of the bed. It bounced the reflection of my uterus framed by my wide bottom to the mirror behind the bed. Between contractions (like viewing a car accident) I felt compelled to stare at my portrait in amazement. I was mortified by the endless string of repeated images and shocked to see myself from that particular angle. It felt too intimate for even me to witness. I bet if I focused harder I could have seen my tonsils.

Feeling great burning, with tremendous force I bore down, emitting a loud high-pitched groan from the back of my throat. My physician—a male, might I add—shushed me. By God, I was literally working my tail off. Are you kiddin' me? How *dare* he SHUSH me! I don't think men are even qualified to be obstetricians. I think they should have to be a member of the Ovarian Club to have a true understanding of and compassion for the incredible pain it induces.

Lucky for the doc I couldn't see his face behind the umpire mask and catcher's mitt. When I tried to thrust myself up to wring his neck, it caused enough force in my abdomen to project the baby toward the opening. Using every ounce of strength I had, I pushed repeatedly for a complete hour until my muscles were weary and my eyes bloodshot. Doubtful that my birthing equipment would part wide enough, I became impatient.

Finally, with the encouragement of my cheering section I pushed so hard I blasted out the baby's head, shoulders and elbows all at once, causing my body to tear wide open like a child ripping open a package of fruit snacks. I was parted like the Red Sea. Holy mackerel! I started with O's in this tic-tac-toe game; I had just become the X's.

Out shot my squiggly, purple, milky-covered, screaming alien that at a glance resembled its ultrasound photos from months earlier. My jelly belly jiggled with delight and the scale immediately tipped in my favor.

I felt relief and happiness beyond measure to see that my baby appeared healthy. Once cleaned up it was joyous to meet and cuddle my beautiful, new, precious and innocent little child. Birth is truly a miracle and I felt blessed to be a mother. Babies are worth every stretch mark.

At this point, I felt like I had bonded with the hospital staff. While the doctor was stitching up my newly remodeled two-family condo, I talked about the next baby. The *next* baby? Now Daddy looked pale. My doctor laughed and claimed that was the first time that a woman was talking about repeating the performance so soon after delivery, even before the stirrups had been removed from the scene. That was the other element that was a miracle…Nature numbs the pain so we forget quickly how miserable it really was.

Childbirth was wonderful, exciting and thrilling. But natural? Not by a long shot! I felt proud to say I delivered my baby with no help from pain-reducing drugs. That was either morbidly brave or satanically stupid. Then when it was all over my husband said to me, "I'm so proud of you, Bonnie, you made it look so easy." Easy! I didn't want it to look easy. I wanted it to look as treacherous as it was so I could hang it over his head for quite some time. *What do you mean you need clean shirts, I already gave you children! What more do you want from me?*

*　　*　　*　　*　　*　　*　　*

Childbirth is the hardest work I have ever done in my life. I have given birth to four babies and I can't honestly say it ever got easier as I was told it would. Women are extraordinarily brave and strong for enduring nine uncomfortably long months, surviving the tremendous pain that birthing children causes, and incredibly still have the strength left to raise them. Mothers are in a league of their own. Our children instinctively cause us to love more deeply than we ever thought possible.

When you have children, every day is Mother's Day, and by gosh, we deserve to celebrate it more than once a year!

CHAPTER 6
Motherhood: You're in for a Wild Ride

The more kids you have, the lower the odds are of their stars aligning, them having dispositions that match or their moods swinging on the same pendulum. I was the fourth child and "the baby" in my family when I was growing up. As a teen, I always teased my mother that I didn't believe anyone would have four children on purpose. She being the good Christian woman that she is means I'll never get it out of her even if it might be the truth. But I did prove the theory wrong by having four children of my own, on purpose!

Life is a roller coaster in general but with each child entering at different times it adds great challenge. Each in separate cars, so to speak, they bring an individual perspective and attitude. Whether they sit in the front seat with arms held up high in the air, laughing and daring the conductor to go faster, or following in the back-seat with eyes closed, screaming and clutching their puke bag— trust me, it's going to be an emotional ride!

One kid can be feverishly fighting diaper rash while another is combative with acne. One is repulsed by girls who seem to carry the plague while the other can't get enough dirty magazines stuffed under his mattress without it altering his deep pocket sheets. One is menstruating with cramps and hiding behind swollen breasts, trying to find herself, while another is going through the hopeful impatient training bra phase and tweaking them daily trying to make them grow. One toddler may have new molars cutting through their gums and having a drop of whiskey rubbed on may soothe the pain; while one teen has metal braces cutting through their gums and pleads for the whiskey remedy. One adolescent is sneaking around trying to tattle on anyone for anything, while another is sneaking around just trying to figure out what they can get away with. It's quite funny when this happens at precisely the same time.

One repels the opportunity and refuses to go to the spring dance while another sits home alone in tears with her fairy godmother trying to turn flip-flops into glass slippers, praying that the invitation will come. One is wetting the bed while I'm anxiously wetting the passenger seat during the driver's ed training of another.

Each child works at his own pace and her own level of motivation. They each strive for very different goals and accomplishments. Sometimes it's not even apparent until they are grown if they have any motivation or will strive for anything in particular. One needs the results of good grades; another child refuses to color within the lines. One youth wants to go out and save the world while another wants to catch and keep every creature in a dirty mayonnaise jar, usually resulting in an unintentional suffocation.

Discipline is completely personalized. One adolescent complies with a mere suggestion of it. All they need is a stern look and a raised hand implying that their butt will hurt if the two make contact. They just drop right down into a chair, covering the target, and promise to be good. One rebel may defy immortality. Test and teeter on every boundary that is set, break and bend every rule laid down and smirk at me the same way I smirked at my parents just to watch them implode. But be careful how you chose to discipline your child because anything you do will most likely end up as an entry in their writing journal one day.

For one teen his room is merely a temporary place to pile his shoes, store his bike parts, drop his dirty laundry around the base of the hamper and leave loose change, with little reason to even open a window shade. To another it is her space that personifies her being. Her room is brightly decorated with personality, displaying collages of artwork and collections of treasures, and the revolving door swirls constantly as the meet-and-greet place for many peers.

One offspring may be here merely to take time to smell the roses. They are so laid-back they collect dust. Most tasks are too big so why even start. They are content to be as lazy as a rug and nonproductive yet their head is full of ideas waiting to happen. R&R is a lifestyle. They like everything to stay right where they left it, so that no matter how much time has passed between uses, it will still be there if and when they need it again. Their motto: Why wash it if you are going to wear it again and why put it away if you are going to use it again?

We parents are along for the coaster ride of our lives when we have children. This ride offers thrills beyond measure that'll rattle every nerve and hair-raising suspense that'll cause the pigment in our hair to slowly disappear. Abrupt tilts and turns can alter our tolerance and patience. Yet it is appealing enough that the great majority of parents come back to the ticket booth, repeatedly!

Being a mom is both gratifying and tiring. In a crowd of thousands a mother can focus on her precious child's face as all the others fade from view. In a lineup she'll lie and say she doesn't recognize anyone. A mom will often sacrifice so that her kids can have more than she ever dreamed of. Motherhood provides a love and a purpose that can't be duplicated in any other profession. Though I can't imagine I would have ever compiled a résumé for any position that was so thankless, provided so little pay and offered such lousy, sleep-deprived hours.

Not to mention the only retirement benefits are that I hope to God my kids have the decency to take me in when I am old and return the favor of wiping my drool and changing my diaper.

I feel amazing pride watching them develop and relief knowing that eventually they will grow up into real people. At times they make me burst with joy and cause laughter until it hurts. I especially feel satisfaction when one of them recites something back to me that I know I said in the first place which means they were listening all along (while pretending not to). Sometimes I feel frustrated, watching them struggle, and wish life wasn't such a challenge.

I have guided my children to become strong individuals who stand up for themselves and what they believe in. Because of that I've run the risk of having our opinions differ at times, them possibly voting against my political party or rooting for an opposing team. But by far the most painful is observing them make choices I know are doomed to fail, which makes my heart ache. At times, I hover nearby to soften any fall and celebrate with exuberance when they succeed.

Eventually they have come to value my opinions and not contradict me just to be argumentative. They have come to admit they need and value me. Occasionally my kids will offer a non-provoked thank you, which means so much. Even when I thought, with my head deep inside the horrendous diaper pail, there could *never* be enough thanks!

Sometimes I am proud that they follow in my footsteps; other times I hope the apple not only falls from the family tree but rolls way down the hill. I pray they have received only the good genes and that the bad ones are what was expelled in afterbirth. I want the best for them and very few fish in the sea are ever good enough.

No matter how old or adamantly independent they become, our job is never done. We have indestructible maternal instinct and a sixth sense. We provide protective care that can be compared to that of a lioness and can be almost deadly if you hurt our young. We never stop worrying about their safety, praying for their good health and wishing for enough happiness for them to reach the stars! I take my position very seriously. It's a privilege and an honor and I feel blessed I am a woman. We are a special breed and the camaraderie between women is universal.

God was very deliberate when he made Eve on the second day. After he made Adam, he gave himself an opportunity to make corrections, change the prototype to near perfection—then he created a woman!

As for the roller coaster, if you invested in a ticket you are in for a wild and memorable ride. Keep your arms and legs in at all times and wait until the car has come to a complete stop for the ride to be over. Caution: It is not for the weak of heart or feeble-minded. If you feel faint, put your head between your knees and blow. The irony for many of us women is that we have evolved right back to the same position we were in delivering them here! All aboard!

Who knew, when he asked to take you for a sexual ride,
the results could be this wild—or last a whole
6,570 days from birth to adulthood—with
very little coasting!

CHAPTER 7
Change of Life May Cause Change of Underwear

Recently, I saw an *Oprah* show discussing menopause. It confirmed that women in the Ovarian Club go through some astounding changes in their hormonal makeup through the years and it is just another reason why we deserve a medal. It's yet another change of life. Like we haven't gone through enough changes already! I recall some startling changes myself. Beginning with breast transformation, cyclical bloating like a beluga whale and the unpredictable Personality Modification Syndrome (PMS) without warning, for starters. Progressing to fertile and abundantly fruitful ovaries producing enormous protruding abdomens and uterine cavities, that provide a disproportionately sized opening to deliver a human being. A woman's user-friendly body and emotional status travels a psychosomatic drama through a litany of challenging tests and tasks only to be left exhausted and unappreciated in the end. Quite frankly, my body has been to hell and back, repeatedly! I have proven to be as adaptable as a chameleon and as accommodating as a reusable party balloon. Yet at this point in my life a little dribble of incontinence from an unexpected sneeze is about all the surprise I can handle.

But this change is apparently bigger than anything we have seen or experienced thus far. This is *The* Change. Not just any old change; it is in fact the real deal. It's when we start to digress and go backwards. Like when the engines of a plane stall in mid-air and you're just kind of free-falling—there's a scary and uncertain pause. That pretty much sums it up. I think it is the pause before we start regressing, ever so slowly, back into men. Hence the term: Men O

Pause. Apparently girls, the rib we had from Adam was on loan, and much to our chagrin, he wants it back.

Many women as they age are plagued by osteoporosis. Shrinkage is the obvious result from removing bone from one's ribcage. Now nieces and nephews approach me using a hand motion showing measurement above me. They pat me on top of my head and say, "The last time I saw you, you were this tall," to prove their statement. I sit on an outdated phonebook, disguised under a cushion, as a booster seat when I drive so I can see over the dashboard. I know my bones have become dense with sediment. My digital scale tells no lies. But how can it be that I keep getting smaller and my weight keeps getting bigger?

Unbalanced gland secretion (which sounds so gross! I find it hard to admit that I actually secrete anything) wreaks havoc on our systems, and as changes and depletion of hormones occur, the signs begin to erupt. Some are definite. Middle-aged women are resorting to comb-over hairdos, trying to disguise their thinning hair like little old men.

Many females I know have gained little Santa bellies, impossible to lose, and experience less desire to curtail their flatulence after years of daintiness and clenched butt cheeks. Though there would be some relief, I'm sure, in finally being able to relax and let loose, I forever try to hang on to my dignity and still attempt to bottle it all up. Thank goodness females don't stoop as low as scratching their private parts in public like our male counterparts.

For other women *The* Change can be an extremely long and subtle process. I have found myself in the fetal position more than once, curled up on the bathroom floor sobbing an endless gush of tears that seemed as heartfelt as anything I've ever experienced. All because someone said my macaroni and cheese was too saucy. Now you know as well as I do that the best part of macaroni and cheese is the sauce. But on certain days reality just seems to get a little cloudy. It is best when these episodes happen in the privacy of your own bathroom, but there are no guarantees.

Heaven forbid if someone should spill milk on the wrong day, place or time. It could send me into a tailspin and nobody would know what hit us. Against my mother's advice about not crying over spilt milk I would sputter uncontrollably while following the trail and wiping it up on my hands and knees. Under a table in a restaurant, with feet dangling in my face, I would sop up tear-diluted milk and blubber incoherently about if only I'd have gone to nursing school this somehow would have never happened. The waiter with a mop in his hand would beg me to come out from under the table next to ours, and insist that he'd take care of it. Looking to avoid further meltdowns, my kids opted to drink out of sippy cups until they were almost eleven.

It took me years to see the pattern, but I did figure out that I needed a mental health day at least once a month. I'd fix me a soup bowl of ice cream smothered in peanut butter sauce with milk chocolate chips piled on top (or any other chocolate I could sniff out hidden in the cupboard). Then I'd apply an artful squirt of whipped cream on each spoonful of sinfully delicious attitude adjustment. We girls sure know how to have fun, don't we?

Curled up on the couch, watching a sad movie, dressed in my frumpiest outfit and moofy slippers while covered in my big furry blanket; let the therapy begin. With a diet soda chaser and a tube of acne cream nearby for the morning after. I'll be damned if I'd have to pay a therapist to get to the bottom of these crisis periods. I have been self-diagnosing for years. I'll cry it out, whatever it is!

Then there's the edgy and irritability stage. You know when

your family (your cherished loved ones) become those you refer to as the "people" I live with. It may be that one of them just rubs you the wrong way, or maybe having to replace the empty paper towel roll with a new one for the sixth time since Sunday could just about send you to the edge. I play fair. I usually warn those around me, "I'm really not in the mood today." Or better yet I'd go into my bedroom for some space, to be alone so I won't lash out or say anything hurtful to anyone that I don't really mean. They are clueless, I tell you! These idiotic people follow me into my room, crowd around me and have the audacity to ask, "Why are you being so cranky?" Quite frankly I don't know why! But should they really be provoking the lion by sticking their limbs into her cage? I don't think so! They are taking their lives into their own hands. My defense attorney will have me plead Menopausal Meltdown and if there are enough women on the jury they will understand exactly why I snapped!

My doctor suggested I could take a little green pill every day as a mood stabilizer to get through this phase. I didn't think it was really necessary. After months of thunderous hissing from the lioness my family sat me down for an intervention. They even offered to give me a ride to the pharmacy and pay for the tablets. Agreeing to try the witch's brew, the remedy also includes a warning label and a list of side effects. Prescription may cause suicidal thoughts or violent actions! Are you kiddin' me? If you ask me we were better off without the added help of the magical green therapy. Now we have to take roll call and count heads every morning to see if the pill is working—and that we're all present. We're all glad it's just a phase that will end—someday.

One day I had a sore throat and was trying to inspect it in the mirror. My head thrown back at an angle, I confirmed the redness in my throat but it was then that I caught a glimpse of a long, coarse hair under my chin. Oh my gosh, testosterone is on the rise! It was a dark, burly whisker thick enough to braid a rug. Then I found another stubbly one just peeking through farther down my neck. Well, that might explain my recent hankering for catnip.

I was horrified that someone must have seen it there and in disbelief that I hadn't observed it sooner. I furiously ran my fingertips up and down the length of my neck in search for others. I rolled and stretched skin from under my chin up over my jaw line, inspecting every inch. I plucked anything that resembled the beginning of lumberjack stubble. So now this old mare has to do a regular inspection for lumpy breasts and gray hairs *and* do sprouting whisker patrol. If I find hair on my back, I'll just die!

When I was in a holistic and natural stage as a teenager I had an aversion to women dyeing their hair. I thought it was fake and phony. I claimed I would never resort to that. I was sure I would accept my gray hair with a greater self-confidence. To hell with that! Now I'm confident that I will do whatever I have to in order to cover my premature gray. Because no matter what age gray hair appears it is always premature and certainly way too early for us to be either prepared for it or deserving of it. I'm not ready to look in the mirror and see my mother. I love her dearly and don't get me wrong, she's a good-looking woman. I'm just not ready to look like her—not just yet anyway! Still, I admire women who have the guts to face and wear their age.

My doctor has warned me of upcoming hot flashes. I welcome them. My flawed internal thermometer constantly leaves me with cold feet and brittle fingers. So I could use a good warming up without the aid of a white sweater. Romantically speaking it might help if I could tear off at least a layer or two. I marvel at Alaskan women. That's got to be some hot guy, to talk you out of your parka when it's thirty degrees below zero and get you to roll around on an ice floor. Count me out. My fur-lined panties, mukluks and bear-skin nightie are staying put.

On Kelly Ripa's show, (oh, I mean Oprah) they discussed how common forgetfulness is and explained signs of reduced mental clarity during the *big change*. Well, I was so happy to hear that piece of information and quite frankly a bit relieved. Those around me have started to question if it is the dementia stage for me. Even I began to wonder if I was losing my sanity, one little piece at a time. Now I no longer have to be concerned when I forget to change out of my bowling shoes at the alley and don't realize I'm still wearing them. It's only while shopping at the grocery store on the opposite end of town on my way home from bowling league that I notice the florescent lights shining upon the glossy stripes of my shoes. I'll just wear them back next week. No one will ever know.

It's amazing how quickly your family will turn on you. How do you like that? They are so quick to remind me when I do something crazy or forget things. But what about all of the things I've remembered? I have memorized all of the NFL teams. What about the extra bonus points I should get for all of those? Just because I have a collection of bowling shoes in my closet is no reason to hint about Alzheimer's or gingko pills.

I'll admit, every once in awhile my mind can play tricks on me. The pleasant term for this is called a "senior moment." However my age doesn't legitimately qualify yet. I don't think running out of gas because there was a glare on the dashboard and I couldn't see the warning light is being senile. For goodness sake, it only happened a few times. Besides, the only way I'll agree to being called a senior is if I get a discount on something or a parking pass in the front row.

Recently I went to a fundraising benefit that held casino-style gambling. With the cost of our admission came fake money to gamble to our hearts' delight. There also was an auction going on to raise additional donations. Getting caught up in the excitement of the event and a gutsy spending frenzy, it wasn't until my hand was raised and my highest bid was accepted that I realized I had no other (real) money along. The wealth of Monopoly dollars in my hand was clearly not sufficient to cover the cost of the item on which I was bidding. It was an honest mistake that anyone could make, right? I'll admit there was some mental numbness involved but hardly dementia! My ever-changing body and mind might be going once, going twice, but it's not yet gone. By the way, the opening bid for the Elvis lampshade with swivel base is eighty dollars. Do I hear eighty-five?

As for PMS, whether it is pre, present or post menstrual, we pretty much have the whole calendar covered. My advice is to keep all firearms and ammunition locked away carefully. Why they don't allow women on the battlefield is beyond me. It could provide extraordinary public safety for our country and a purely thera-peutic exercise for the ladies. We should come with a warning label. BEWARE: She may detonate at any moment with little warning or provocation due to an unresolved issue she has been harboring for quite some time. This too shall pass. Give her plenty of love, patience and respect. Treat her kindly, for she has been to hell and back and may take you with her next time. She has had to deal with a lot of frustration and "Change." It's not her fault!

As my grandmother used to say, "So late oldt, we get so schmart!" I'm sure some of the quote has been lost in translation over the years but I sure have come to love the saying. We do get older, but, more importantly, wiser with age. Unfortunately, we now have the answers to so many questions that never seem to get asked. And our heads are so full to capacity with information that we may seem confused and overwhelmed at times. Rightly so. Imagine what's all in there. I wish I had the ability to filter out some of the obsolete and unwanted information crammed in there from the past. For example if I could sift out my ex-husband's birth date or his hemorrhoid cream brand (which both make me think of an ass) I'd probably be able to remember my ATM pin number. At times my mind goes blank in the dark bank alley, while a parade of rambunctious party-goers pile up behind me waiting their turn in the next car. Maybe I should just use the word "ass" as my password code instead, since that seems to come to mind so often.

On the beauty front, there is a constant battle because we are losing elasticity and moisture. I believe this to be true, as my chamois-like skin soaks up half of the water in the tub before my bath is complete. I need to rise earlier than ever before; I like to stand on my head which circulates blood and helps smooth wrinkles for a fresher appearance. The next phase will be Bondo. My cells sponge up the eight glasses of water a day and my fingers retain water like little sausages, yet gravity still gets the best of me. Before bed I moisturize every inch of my body, wear lip balm and still have to file and smooth some rough edges with a belt sander by morning. If I ever forget this ritual one night you just might find a dried-up prune on my pillow at daybreak.

Fashion can also be an added challenge as we age. We are the ones who keep lobbying the fashion industry for elastic waist bands to come back. We need more than bras to lift and separate. The twins hang down staring at the floor all day and our droopy cleavage means our low-neck blouse is slit almost to our navels causing the empire waistline to hit at approximately hip level. Everything starts to shift south and even our arches may begin to fall.

Women have innocently been bombarded with hormonal imbalance, causing whiskers, forgetfulness, thinning hair, disappearing bone mass, incontinence and emotional instability. People should cut us girls some slack and certainly we who possess ovaries should support each other with admiration and understanding. The inner works of our biological clock ticks loudly and our expiration date is practically stamped on our foreheads. Any eggs left behind are merely omelet quality. I am grateful that when our parts fail to perform and eggs misfire, we can do it somewhat discreetly. When a man's jewel loses its luster, it just hangs there, pathetically limp, and obvious for all to see. Men might be capable of producing sperm until a very mature age but let's face it those little senior swimmers are not so spry, by the time they do the backstroke all that way, they are just praying they find an egg to cling onto merely as a life-saving device.

Go ahead, Adam, you can have your rib back if you must—but that won't hurt our spirit. The female species will still be at an advantage with the extra parts that makes us superior! We will deal with the adversity of infiltrated testosterone and depleting estrogen. We will conquer the challenge as we have all the other stages of our lives. This Change will be our grandest of all and we will fight to hang onto our femininity until the end. To paraphrase the famous song, "We are women, hear us roar!"

I advise you to follow your doctor's recommendations and remember to take your supplements accordingly to level out your imbalance. Warning: Don't ignore the signs or pause too long—or the results could be devastating. If you experience the urge to scratch your crotch, the sprouting of a penis, or notice hair growth on your once smooth rear-end, it may be too late!

Cut out and hang where it can be most beneficial to the greatest number of people!

<u>BEWARE:</u>

She may detonate at any moment with little warning or provocation due to an unresolved issue she has been harboring for quite some time. This too shall pass. Give her plenty of love, patience and respect. Treat her kindly, for she has been to hell and back and may take you with her next time. She has had to deal with a lot of frustration and "Change."

It's not her fault!

Part 2
Maternally Speaking

CHAPTER 8
Motherboard

As far back as my babysitter course graduation I can remember people continually asking me to ponder my career options. My brilliant response was usually quite consistent but indecisive. My choices were to become a nurse, a teacher, a mother or to become the first president to possess breasts and a uterus. The older I grew the decision became more apparent.

I'm far too passive and naïve to be political. My solutions would be very simplistic but practical. My rules would include no war with bullets, just paintballs! No international problems would exist. We must respect each other but if we don't get along, especially with other countries, we are grounded and must stay in our own yards! Violence would not be tolerated. People would have to work out their grievances in bumper cars! When the economy was unbalanced, print more money! No one would get anything until there was enough to be shared equally, with everyone! All people would have to be kind to each other and get along, or else! And a raised hand, a fiery look in the eyes and the fear of "Or Else" would be enough to keep everyone in line! Do I have your presidential vote? Probably not!

I am very curious and intrigued with science and our amazing bodies. I also have a compassionate flair for caring for others. I don't get jittery about bodily fluids as long as they are kept on the inside where they belong. However, my feeling of faintness when blood escapes to the outside of the body cavity, whether it is a drop, a smudge, a trickle, squirting, gushing or a pool, sometimes gets the best of my nerves! It makes a mess and the stains are impossible to get out. Throughout my life, I have tried hard to avoid anything pertaining to an abscess, oozing pus or anything causing a hemorrhage. Fine; I'm a coward. Honestly, I don't think I can get over the yuk factor when it comes to feet either! My squeamishness could very well be a deterrent to a nursing career. Scratch that one off the list.

I have such a love of children and find it rewarding to be able to shape their little sponge-like minds. Fostering and teaching other people's children would be very rewarding but did not seem complete somehow as you have to send them home at the end of the day. And maybe that is precisely what keeps teachers going! My selfish instinct was that I wanted to have my own children and spend all day with them!

My yearning to have a baker's dozen of children was definite and my libido grew stronger with each ovulation. My new unsuspecting husband came along in his prime, blinded by an insatiable sexual urge. I was a young bride with lots of fertile and eager eggs. Enthusiastically my mission began.

I married young, four days short of twenty in fact, which I absolutely would not advise anyone to do, even if it seemed like a grand idea at the time. The only exception might be if you lived in the fifteenth century and you were to marry Prince Charming with the offerings of a castle, carriage, servants, cook and a featherbed. However, we've never really heard the ending to that story and I would bet that even Cinderella was disappointed and disillusioned when Mr. Charming failed to do his fair share of paternal tasks.

I had watched my mom for years. She always appeared happy and content being a homemaker. It seemed that she had a laundry basket propped on her hip 66% of the time, and her hands were in the kitchen dish water the remainder of the time. But Mom was always cheerful. *Who wouldn't want that?* I thought. So I wanted to follow in her footsteps.

My husband and I had three children in the first five years which were well spaced in my opinion. Boy, girl, boy! We had a false alarm once between the first and second births and an additional thrill in thinking I was pregnant with twins during the third pregnancy. I was so excited at the notion of having twins and cried when the doctor discovered there was really only one baby in there. I think my son Bradley really received the energy (and equaled the challenge) of two, but arrived in a single body, nonetheless.

I was ecstatic being a mom to my three youngsters. I loved my role as activity director and eventually our house became *the* place to play in the neighborhood. We had the playground equipment, sandbox, kiddie pool, games, art projects and snacks. We had to turn kids away when we wanted family time to ourselves. I could have made a fortune if I'd charged admittance.

Being a stay-at-home mom afforded me the flexibility to continue my joyful job as a late-night comedienne for awhile. It was my only real link to adults at that point in my life. Spending my weekends in front of adult bottle-fed audiences wasn't always as glamorous as one might think, though. Some days I truly preferred the companionship of my young playmates, riding scooters, running through the sprinkler and finger-painting to the occasional belligerence of an obnoxious, disgruntled, late-night patron who merely wanted to hear filth, which I just couldn't deliver.

How could I have known at the ripe age of nineteen what I really wanted in life? But while our ten years of marriage had not only confirmed what I wanted for myself and my children, it surely solidified what I didn't want. After years of marital deterioration we succumbed to the fact that divorce was inevitable. Our directions were opposite and our hopes and dreams came from two different galaxies. Our expectations were shattered by reality. My parents made a loving marriage look so easy and attainable. I always thought that love could conquer all. I was wrong.

Our lives and my mothering role have changed immensely through the years. Before the divorce, I had successfully been a homemaker with my floors scrubbed and knickknacks dusted every Friday like clockwork. We played, had snack time and the kids had scheduled naps. A nutritious, three-course meal hit the table every evening by six and the bedtime ritual was precise and orderly.

Then, after the divorce there I was, alone, with three kids—and basically the shit hit the fan.

As a single woman I was thrust into the working-mom role, where I learned all too quickly what it was like to be broke and exhausted. Mornings became chaotic trying to get everyone delivered to their destination on time, in more or less a presentable outfit, including me. And a couple of times, I am embarrassed to admit, I was so overworked and frazzled that I actually forgot to pick up my descendants from daycare. The director had to call and remind me they were closing and my kids would be waiting on the sidewalk.

Cutting corners became an art. Walking became an activity, not just exercise. Hanging clothes outside was the new term for "dry cleaning." Renting one pair of skates in a three-hour period meant each of the kids got a one-hour time slot for fun, all to him or herself. I had to fill my kids up with milk to make two Happy Meals stretch to feed three children. But we could eat a full day's worth of free food samples loitering around the grocery store on Saturdays.

Making ends meet wasn't easy. I got us held captive in a parking structure more than once by not having enough money in my wallet to pay for our release. And one time I panicked in the toll-booth between two states, staring at the eighty-seven cents in my possession. Thank goodness for the loose change collection that always seemed to appear (during emergencies) under the back-seat of our car.

In some areas my standards had to lower due to supply and demand. There was only one of me to go around. Light bulbs that blew had to wait until there was enough darkness to warrant dragging the ladder in. Due to the lack of time required to remove webs that had accumulated in the corners of my house, I had to learn that spiders are our friends. I made folding laundry a contest. I could hardly stay awake through a game of Candy Land, and bedtime generally didn't occur without yelling and disorder of some kind. But all in all I'm proud to say we were happy, well-adjusted and appreciative of what we had (mostly each other) and the dreams were sweet nonetheless.

Then I took on the new chapter of remarriage. Never being sure I was complete with my three-ring circus I contemplated having another baby with my new husband who hadn't any of his own offspring. I stated I was willing but at thirty-eight years of age surely my eggs had a biological shelf life and were doomed to expire if not hatched in a timely manner. Time was of the essence.

Being pregnant at an older age didn't concern me until every doctor, nurse, intern, pharmacist, radiologist and nutritionist told me what a high-risk category I was in, but always followed with a "Don't worry." Thanks a lot. I wasn't worried until they induced their anxious attitude on me for Pete's sake. Come on, at thirty-eight I thought I was still in my prime!

My kids at that point were seventeen, fifteen and twelve. It was brilliant; instant babysitters. The announcement that I was having another child didn't come as a shock to all who knew me but the responses were similar amongst most: "More power to you," and "Better you than me!"

Everything went relatively smoothly as I was determined to show everyone that the late thirties are the new twenties!

My kids loved feeling the fetus kicking and the hiccups that shook my abdomen. The option for my two teenagers to be included in the birth was extended as the date crept closer. We were all thrilled about having an addition to the family, and what better way could Mom extend the birth control message to teenagers, than by having them see the drama for themselves?

We piled into the car as if going to Disneyland for an experience of a lifetime. And that it was. It was a horribly intense labor and I so desperately wanted to show them how tough I was to handle all of the pain. Not very successfully might I add. As the baby's head was crowning my oldest son Ryan was flustered and still undecided whether or not he wanted to stay in the room for the actual delivery or join his brother Brad who was in the waiting room with his suitcase of toys, videos and snacks to keep him occupied.

I didn't really want the portrait of my vagina burned into my son's memory bank for the rest of his life so the plan was to have Ryan present for the overall miraculous birthing experience but out of eyeshot of any gruesome parts that could ultimately ruin him for life. Baby was coming, stirrups were going up and the room's motion halted. Hastily the nurse asked him twice, "Are you in or out?" His indecisiveness caused him to be shoved in the corner, stunned and confused. My daughter Nicole at the head end of the bed was calm but in awe. At least one thing was for sure; my birth control scare tactic had worked!

Because I have experienced being a young mom, once I showed up to a school conference and the teacher asked if I was my daughter's babysitter. Because I have experienced being an old(er) mom, I showed up to a school conference and the teacher thought my son brought his grandma.

I now have four children that span a whole generation. By the time I get the fourth one to the legal age at which I can contemplate moving away without offering a forwarding address, I will have been in the first phase of mothering for a total of thirty-five—long years. That's just not right, is it? Again you're thinking, "Sucks to be you!" But it is what it is, and I love my role! Thanks to many of us trendsetters we have changed the concept of what a new-age traditional family model can be.

Aside from being a woman which is an amazing hormonal feat all by itself, many of us choose the vocation of motherhood. I lost count of the number of times I've asked myself through the years, "What was I thinking!" In hindsight, though, I can't imagine my life without my ancestral creations. It is I who have molded them into who they are today and they in turn have made me complete.

My children have actually allowed me to fulfill all of my career choices. As their teacher of life I have taught them all that I know. Whether or not they followed my advice may be a different story. As their nurse I have mended many physical injuries and nurtured numerous emotional hurts. Funny, when they feel pain on the outside we try to keep all the ooze to stay inside and when they are hurting on the interior we try to pull it all out of them. Lastly, as their household president (yes, with breasts and a fine uterus) I governed, oftentimes being the referee, judge and jury. They don't even realize how lucky they should be that it was a hung jury.

It was their cuteness that saved their lives, many times!

CHAPTER 9

"Hey Bonnie, Where's Clyde?"

Waiting with anticipation, palms begin to sweat. The room is small and the air is still. Knees are still a bit weak from hovering over the porcelain throne. An abundant supply of warm, liquid gold waits in a Dixie cup specimen holder. The sophisticated, pink plastic dip-stick is lowered in strategically as if the angle could somehow make a difference. Eyes fixated on the clear panel on the side of the pregnancy testing device which holds the answer that will secure your future—one way or another!

The clock ticks so slowly. Each passing second is a collage of uncertain thoughts.

Tick: Yeah, I always wanted to be pregnant before my sister!

Tock: Darn, we should have waited a month so I could be off for the summer!

Tick: I'll have to breast feed because I can't afford formula!

Tock: Cool, my boobs will get big!

Tick: Crap! Now I can't get drunk at my best friend's wedding next month!

Tock: I'm going to put lotion on right away so I don't get those weird zebra-striped stretch marks!

Tick: Perfect! My niece is almost old enough to babysit!

Tock: Dang, I hope my butt doesn't get big!

Tick: Oh no, I wanted to finish my degree!

Tock: I'll never let my baby suck its thumb and ruin its teeth!

Tick: I'm tough; I'm going to have this baby naturally!

Tock: Since I couldn't be, I hope my child will be president!

Tick: I'm not even sure what colic is!

Tock: Cool! Now I get to buy some new clothes!

Tick: If it's a girl I still have my first pair of roller skates in the attic!

Tock: Damn it! I think I already gained weight!

Tick: If it's a boy I will insist he learn how to scrub a toilet!

Tock: What if it has bright red hair like my cousin?

Ding! The timer chimes a stroke of reality. It's the two pale blue line method. For that particular brand that means a fruitful conception! Almost immediately following the elated excitement or the hysterical quandary is the stage of reflection in which to ponder, "What shall we name our baby?" Let the quest begin!

Some go out on a limb to choose Biblical names for their offspring, even when their religious convictions seem a mystery to everyone around them. Using Biblical names may test your faith, however. History may repeat itself. Example: be prepared to get a call from your little Mary someday: "Mom, I'm pregnant and I'm not sure how it happened!"

Using a great name won't ensure greatness but it is worth a try. Your baby Moses is destined to be a leader and world traveler. Thank goodness we now have GPS so at least he won't get lost in the desert for forty years! And, well, no matter how confident you are that your son will be a brilliant carpenter, it's the walking on water that only one divine being has mastered. Avoid the name "Jesus" for it has been done to perfection and is a hard act to follow.

Some parents think the answers are in the stars. They like to name their children after their strong and bold zodiac signs. This may be what guides their personality, directs their destiny and helps them to choose a partner. Example: the register continues to ring up the expensive price tags as my young "Taurus" crashes his way through the delicate china shop.

Some parents research their deep-rooted genealogy and are guided by historical names on the family tree. Other variations are following in a respected, loved one's footsteps, but who you're pretty sure your child will never quite live up to. Example: Junior.

Choosing a member from your ancestry who was so great and important is a nice gesture but if they lack a little individuality, one may became a number. Example: Mickey Mouse III.

One popular method is looking for meaning through word interpretation. Example: The Greek meaning for Bonnie is "a happy flower." Makes you happy just thinking about it, doesn't it? But I haven't quite figured out what the hell "My Bonnie lies over the ocean" means.

Looking for an ethnic following is empowering. But it can be equally awkward or slightly politically incorrect to ignore those unwritten guidelines, however. Example: a blond, curly-haired, freckle-faced, blue-eyed boy named Kunta?

Choosing a name of someone you already admire. However, some are of such uniqueness, they should not be copied. Example: Santa or Jesus (which has already been mentioned but bears repeating).

Some think rhyming is cute or believe all of their children should have a binding theme. Example: Connie, Ronnie, Bonnie, Donnie.

Others prefer a common communal letter so they are easier to remember. Example: Kris, Kurt, Kim, Kip, Kay.

Always experiment with the letters to see what the initials will become. Example: Andrew Steven Sullivaneer = A.S.S. (which could ruin a kid for life).

Traditionally, expectant parents search through volumes of baby books to find the perfect name that will infuse their pride and joy with unlimited potential. It is important to love the name you pick! This also bears repeating: You must LOVE IT!! Because it is a word that will hopefully cross your lips more often than projectile spit-up will land on your favorite blouse.

Choose a name that is of the optimum length. Sometimes short and sweet works well especially on presidential campaign banners and posters. Example: Will Winn.

If a name is too long the font will need to be reduced down which makes it hard to read on certificates of excellence and a Ph.D. diploma. Example: Dr. Bartholomeau O'Schowenberger.

If it is too commonplace it may lack credibility. Example: Joe Blow.

The spelling of a name can be creative but if it's too tricky it will give the recipient a complex forever. He or she will never receive the correct birthday cake or Publisher's Clearing House winner announcement.

A name should be clearly pronounceable in various tones and decibels.

Example: <u>whisper</u>. After the picture had begun, my son wandered down to the front row, in the dark movie theater, whereas I had stopped way back at the sixth row. My hands were loaded with popcorn, red Swedish Fish and two sodas. Four people had stood up (half slouched forward with their jackets bunched in their arms) and waited for us to pass through to our seats in the middle of the row. I emphatically whispered "Alex" in a Darth Vader tone to try to get my child's attention as he made rabbit ears behind people's heads which reflected up onto the big screen.

Example: <u>low roar</u>. My two-year-old daughter had just announced, "I have to go pee now." As I darted down the aisles of the two-acre Wal-Mart Supercenter, three of the four wheels on our cart spun aimlessly. I dodged around other shoppers like we were inside a pinball game, as I desperately tried to get to the bathroom in the farthest corner of the store, before my darling turned into a Little Mermaid swimming in her own sea. In a low roar I suggested that if Nicole could hang on just a bit longer, she would get a treat!

Example: <u>convincing</u>. A brave and theatrical child had impressed his whole fourth-grade class as well as the P.E. teacher by slithering up the thick ropes to the high ceiling of the gymnasium. Tired from holding on, he perched himself up onto the large gray steel girder which ran across the ceiling. He decided he really enjoyed the attention from the onlookers and refused to abide by the teacher's demands that he should come down to safety. The principal had to call his mom to come to school and persuade him down to reality. In a controlled manner she needed to convey her message (without clenching her teeth) so Brian would know that she was the boss. She also had to be convincing enough that he'd believe she wouldn't ground him for life, when he did comply!

Example: <u>commanding</u>. As I balanced on the highest rung of the ladder trying to reach the peak of the cathedral ceiling with my paintbrush I glanced down to see my eager toddler grab hold of the corner of the newspaper that sat on top of the counter. It was shielding the counter surface from the open Sky Blue paint can, wet lid and wooden stir stick. As he stood on the off-white carpet and pulled the paper above his head slowly toward the edge, I let out a commanding order for Bradley to stop. Before the mess could collide with his golden locks and beyond.

Example: <u>demanding</u>. I arrived home after a long day of work. I found my teenage babysitter watching her usual soap operas. Curled up on the sofa she kept her boyfriend's cellular voice close to her ear for commercial-time entertainment. She appeared exhausted and overworked as usual, while she shuffled into her clogs. After I delivered her weary body to her home down the street, I returned to take on my next homemaker/mothering job. I glanced out the kitchen window as I pondered our dinner choices. I saw that the new scooter I had recently financed (so I could give my son just what he wanted for his birthday) was dismantled in ninety-six pieces and scattered across the garage floor with little rhyme or reason. Shocked, I let out a high-pitched scream of rage, aiming to get some attention from my inquisitive and curious child, then demanded an explanation from Ryan (which had somehow turned into a four-syllable name).

Example: <u>pride</u>. As my daughter panted and blew her way through contractions, her legs were in stirrups; her pained look of anguish was one that I could relate to. After what seemed like days of watching my "baby girl" struggle, she pushed and forced out the most beautiful new life only a grandma could imagine. Feeling thrilled and expressing all the pride possible: "Nicole, he's gorgeous!"

Choose names for your children as if it is the biggest gift you give them, aside from life itself. Don't give them a reason to hate you for it. They will find plenty of other things to blame you for.

You better get started. You are going to need all nine months to figure this one out!

CHAPTER 10

The Nipple Is the Tip of the Iceberg

After my first son was born I was elated to be a mom. I did become a bit lonely, however. I was the first of all my friends to be married and birthing offspring. This new little creature had become the center of my axis. My breasts now had a real-life function other than catching popcorn at the movies or being ogled at. I now was a brunette feeding machine. So what went in came out. No more hops and brew for this feed mill. I was up all hours of the night, certainly not due to beer parties and socializing as my friends were.

This was all just fine with me. I was plenty ready to pack away the tapper and keg but my circle of friends really couldn't relate to my happy new lifestyle. I thought it would be nice to meet some other moms who were just as focused on their babies and "into" mothering as I was.

I saw an announcement for a "La Leche League" meeting. The local group was gathering in one of the women's homes. The group's mission is to encourage and support breast-feeding moms and provide parenting companionship. I thought I would like to bond with some fellow mothers so I responded that I would join their meeting. I respect a woman's right to breast-feed but I sure wouldn't be bold enough to share the experience in public. I don't really think the public wants to be involved anyway! But to those women gutsy enough to nurse in the middle of an airport, more power to them. I am a proud but rather private breast-feeder myself.

Anyway, I was excited to actually have a reason to take off my fuzzy slippers, wear something other than stretched-out maternity pants, put on makeup and go out for an evening. I had to plan the whole day in advance so that I had a bottle of milk pumped and ready. I had the feedings spaced out so that I would be gone at the right time to give me an ample window to be away but only miss one feeding. I was happy to have a "date" with the notion of making new friends and socializing with adults. My girlfriends wouldn't be jealous; it was a far cry from doing body shots and dancing at the club, but I was excited just the same to be getting out for a little while.

I arrived, just on time but hurried as always. As I quickly entered the front door which opened right into their living room I immediately felt a sickening feeling. It was a room full of loving, devoted mothers of all ages. But they each had a child in their arms! Oh my God! No one said anything about bringing my baby! The room got quiet as they gawked at their new member who had inattentively failed to bring her child! What kind of tainted, careless estrogen could I have in my veins? My chest was holding in a silent gasp and my cheeks were flushed with embarrassment. In shameful disbelief, I quickly found a seat and tried to quietly plead my case of innocence to nearby mothers who were beaming with joy, cuddling their precious little ones.

"I didn't know we were supposed to bring our babies", I pleaded in a whisper.

I had one more opportunity at redemption when it came time to introduce myself to the crowd. My body slouched as if to hide my empty arms but my cheeks remained blushing red and I had a nervous laugh that was awkward. I really would have loved a beer at that moment. The hostess offered me a choice of fresh carrot juice straight from the juicer or a papaya nectar slushy. Oh boy! What would Ryan want? I wondered. *If he were there!*

Each time the speaker gave a breast-feeding demonstration or suggestion she looked around the room and then focused on me as if to imply I needed extra help or wasn't too bright. The long meeting eventually adjourned and the leader invited us to help ourselves to refreshments which sat on the table across the room.

Before she had finished with her sentence the commotion began. Mothers were adjusting their seating, propping pillows, and hoisting children into their laps. Some kids toddled and some ran in from the next room. Then breasts were flopping out in every direction. That evening, I saw more protruding nipples than in any issue of *National Geographic*. Politely looking in the other direction was impossible. Areolas were staring at me from every direction. There was one woman who needed the whole sofa to breast-feed her child. The kid unbuttoned her blouse for goodness sake and said, "Klim, Mama, klim."

The mother giggled. "That's milk backwards," she explained.

Now, forgive me for being a stickler but I think when your child is old and big enough and has the dexterity to retrieve his own cup from the cupboard, lift a gallon jug to pour his own glass of milk and dunk his own cookies—it is time to wean! The only thought that sustained me from further discomfort at that moment was the hope of getting a big piece of chocolate cake. Maybe even a fudge brownie or some cookies might help to salvage the evening. Looking down at my feet, I sheepishly worked my way across the room to gather something sinfully delicious. There sat dry rhubarb muffins and stark white unbuttered popcorn.

Inconspicuously, I made it to the door and snuck out without a trace. In disbelief, I rushed home to my baby to reassure him and myself that I was a good mom and he wouldn't have wanted to be there anyway! Since there was a pumped bottle of milk, it meant I had an extra four hours to circulate nasty stuff through the milk house and evacuate it before the next feeding. I popped open a cold beer and settled in my rocking chair, nibbling a leftover donut with chocolate icing. Ryan gave me a great toothless smile as I kissed his chubby cheeks. This was the best date I could have asked for and for me, a very sound career choice!

I commend the "La Leche League" of women who devote so much of themselves, unselfishly, to their children. Breast-feeding is a very rewarding, healthy and private bonding experience to have with your child. But for the group feeding frenzy, I'll pass. If I wanted to be ogled, I'd take my girls and go out dancing at the club!

CHAPTER 11
Finders Keepers

A phone call I hoped I'd never have to make in all my life was, "Honey, I lost Junior!"

We're not talking about "I'm sorry I dented the station wagon by backing into a bulldozer" or "Sweetheart, I accidentally left the dry cleaner's with your only newly cleaned and pressed suit on the roof of the car and, well… I kind of drove off and your suit is now a hood ornament on a Mack truck headed for South Dakota."

I'm talking "Honey, I don't know how to tell you this but we won't be needing a new car seat anymore because I lost our only budding branch on the family tree!"

Isn't this every parent's nightmare?

Frantically, I dart about the mall sticking my head into each of the various stores, looking for my misplaced child. I called out his name in a sweet, loving and calm tone just loud enough to be heard above the common shopping noises and ringing of registers, so that my frightened son would hear my voice and return to safety.

Not wanting to cause a scene or alarm any security personnel nearby because then I'd have to explain with embarrassment that as I was gazing through the glass at the fudge shop, I became distracted trying to decide between Double Chocolatey Supreme or Fudgy Nut Melt Away. As I counted to see if the loose change in the bottom of my purse would be enough to satisfy my craving, I lost track of my most prized possession: my toddler!

I scurried pathetically about with my empty umbrella stroller.

My pace quickened to that of a speed walker as I poked my head into the next storefront. I found a less than enthusiastic clerk adorned in pierced baubles and hoops scattered throughout his facial region. He wore a leather choker collar around his neck with spikes protruding outward. It's doubtful his mother dressed him that day!

Taken aback by the green gecko tattooed on his hand, I briefly considered the thought of my pure child confronting that particular clerk. In my mind I questioned whether my child might be severely frightened or awestruck with admiration. Quite frankly, neither of which reactions I wanted from my son.

He jumped, which caused the orange Mohawk atop his head to jiggle, as I yelled to the back of the store hoping to find a more motherly figure, "Have you seen my child?"

He looked dazed and confused and the shake of his head cast off a "No" answer. At that moment, I felt terror. I raced on.

My head was full of thoughts of abduction. I envisioned all sorts of characters who might have taken my little darling. I looked down toward the food court where each and every person looked like a suspect. That moment confirmed how strange strangers can seem.

By then, I was screaming Ryan's name at a decibel that could be heard throughout the seven-acre shopping center, searching for security with my head jerking to and fro like one of those dog figurines on the dashboard of a car.

"Where in the hell are the police when you need them?" I thought.

I glanced to my left where the fountain stood in the atrium. And I saw my hero, a police officer bent over, holding the apple of my eye by his ankles, my son's hands flailing in the water trying to retrieve some fudge money for Mommy. That's my smart boy!

Gleefully, I yelled out my youngster's name one final time. Relieved and tearful, I crouched down next to my precious little one and embraced him with all the love I've ever felt. His wet, dripping little hands clutched our new-found lucky coins.

"Don't ever wander off away from Mommy without telling me where you are going," I scolded in a feeble tone.

With little explanation I profusely thanked the officer who saved the day, our newest candidate to be added to our Christmas letter list. Then we continued on with shopping. By that time, I noticed most store employees' had gathered in their respective doorways. My child had become a celebrity of sorts, known by name to every mall employee within a two-mile radius. We were all relieved my tyke had been discovered.

At home during dinner that evening my husband asked, "Anything exciting happen today?" I decided to wait till later to tell him about the car and his suit. "No, not really," I responded with a shrug. "Would you like some fudge?"

CHAPTER 12

From The Mouths of Babes

Watching my babies' precious facial expressions and funny squinting eyes rolling independently under their eyelids when they slept was entertaining. Their dreams caused their lips to make subconscious and uncontrollable shapes and movements during their naps. It would appear they were chatting with the angels. If only they could talk.

Unfortunately, it would be a long wait before something literal would come out. I repetitively urged, "Say 'Mama.' Can you say 'Mama'?"

I read to them endlessly. I recited words, sang songs and talked my fool head off, prompting them and anxiously awaiting their first word. Come on, all it takes is one consonant and one vowel to make a word. You can do it, baby! However, there were a few phases we undoubtedly had to conquer first.

Nicole as a baby went through a four-week projectile vomiting stage for no apparent reason. But don't let the word "vomit" scare you. With babies, all that goes in is milk, so all that will come out is milk, just slightly curdled. At some point after every meal she would expel slimy hot lava—sour milk—that could spoil anyone's appetite.

It was really quite distasteful for all of us involved so I won't dwell on it but, like any mother does, I have to brag. Her projectory distance was really quite amazing. If I had her propped on my shoulder just right she could clear the rag over my shoulder and send a baptismal shower of splatter on someone's shoes two pews behind us at church. "Peace be with you," I would stammer as I crouched to shine their shoes with a tattered kitchen towel, hoping I wouldn't find ooze between someone's open-toe sandals.

Of course I took her to the doctor to be checked out. He said as long as she was still gaining weight she seemed fine. And her double chin and triple-rolled thighs were proof that she was just fine. We would wait to see what would become of it, he said, but in his opinion she was just going through a gluttonous stage. To me it was strange to have a bulimic baby until I noticed how happy she was. She would eat as much as she could. Then, no matter how delicately I handled her, my little china doll would spit all over everything in sight including me, and grin while she watched me clean up the trail.

A bath towel soon replaced the small kitchen towel for clean-ups, and keeping her in a vinyl blowup wading pool in the living room helped to contain the mess and was easy to spray down. One hiccup could cover her completely when she was in an erect position. She would just give me that toothless, satisfied grin afterward. Her little fingers and toes were starting to wrinkle and prune from the great number of baths she was getting. I became a bit edgy. At every sound she would release I quickly reacted by holding her out away from me as far as my arms would reach. I then got smart and learned to carry her facing away from me. She could really clear a room when people saw her coming and we could get any pew we wanted in church.

Eventually my Miss Piggy stopped gorging herself and learned to eat like a young lady. The horrible and puzzling vomit phase ended nearly as quickly as it developed. I was so glad when it was over and I could cuddle my little one again without feeling like the pin had been pulled on the time bomb and I was waiting for detonation. I also felt relieved she stopped because there had been rumors of an exorcism in the works.

As children grow, their little tongues get to explore new and exciting textures and flavors. My son loved carrots. He couldn't get enough of them. As a mom concerned about his healthy intake I gave him all the veggies he would gum. During a routine check-up his doctor remarked, "Ryan likes carrots, doesn't he?"

Surprised by his magician's abilities, I responded, "Yes, but how did you know that?"

He pointed and said, "Look at him. He's turning orange."

Sure enough, due to the overabundance of vitamin A in his diet, the pigment of his skin was turning him a lovely shade of orange. Oh well, parenting is all about trial and error, with much more emphasis on the latter. But at least Ryan has great eyesight.

Unusually so, my kids loved all the orange foods. My blender was whipping up all sorts of pureed wonders. I learned that sweet potatoes look exactly the same going into a child as they do coming out. And the last food I wanted to be on my child's tongue when he or she had a big sneeze coming on was pureed peaches. It's an unforgettable experience. The sneeze abruptly shot food out the mouth and nose. The peach goo spread like wildfire, staining everything it touched and left a sticky residue on anything in its path, which was usually my face, arms, hair, glasses, and so on. You get the picture, don't you?

Along with mastering new foods there came new and individual sounds that accompanied their developing personalities. Not words just yet. "Can you say Ma Ma Ma Ma Ma ?" I'd babble. I'd have settled for just about anything but I knew it was only a matter of time before I'd start hearing grunts, gurgles, goos, giggles, gasps, high-pitched gleeful noises and growls. Babies and toddlers are just as busy making communicating sounds as they are making teeth.

As for teeth growing in—some do it with little celebration or commotion and others want you to feel their pain. We rub their gums with ointments and ice packs to soothe their discomfort. They gnaw on anything and drool as a constant reminder that they are working on something big. There is no rhyme or reason.

Ryan started drooling profusely around his third month and I expected a tooth any day. It wasn't until he was almost eleven months and toddling around before all of a sudden he opened his mouth and there were his shark teeth. There were rows and rows of them. He produced six teeth within ten days. In one week his menu went from mashed banana and pureed wiener to steak and baked potato.

Nicole started gnawing on my precious nipples early, trying to get teeth to rub their way through. I was about ready to have a mouth-guard made for her or give up on the whole breast-feeding idea completely. I was afraid she was going to cut through me before the tooth would cut through her gums. By three and a half months already she was showing her first sign of a tooth. Ryan and Nicole's are the extreme cases, with the other two kids falling somewhere in between.

A celebration follows when the long-awaited "Mama" is finally blurted out. Perfect pronunciation isn't crucial as long as there is an M and an A and not necessarily in that order. Fumbling through the frustrating babbling stage of young linguists, we all try to decipher what the consonants mean. Certain letters are too tricky to enunciate. R's and T's were very late in coming to my toddlers' vocabulary. Nicole called Ryan "Yiyan" for a long time because she couldn't get the R, and in later years Alex couldn't get the R in "Brad" either. So he would call his big brother "Bad."

I recall one time when Nicole and I made a visit up to the

classy hors d'oeuvres' table during my friend Cathi's wedding reception. We were nearly the last ones to fill our plates and be seated before the best man began to make a toast. In the still of the crowded room my daughter lit up with delight and loudly asked, "Mommy, can I have some big peanus?" as she pointed to the cashews. Jaws dropped and the snickers erupted in the room while many of the women's heads nodded in understanding. We went home and began speech therapy that evening.

Another day the earth moves is when our precious ones test their boundaries and defiantly respond to us with a "No". The first time we gasp and hide our giggle. The second time we cock our head to the side and force a serious face. By the eighth time our patience is challenged, the hair on our neck raises, and with angered and squinting brows, we question our previous birth control choices. We wonder why we taught them to talk in the first place. They're lucky they're so cute; it's saved their lives again!

Finally the recognizable words came. First they trickle, then they gush. The words then form short coherent phrases which grow to be full sentences. Then when you least expect it, a question is formulated. With the satisfaction of getting a response comes yet another question. Then the inquiries become better, tougher and deeper. Some are theoretical, philosophical and even political. Why? Why? Why? Why? Why?

Talking becomes the replacement pastime for drop-the-rattle-and-watch-the-idiot-pick-it-up-and-put-it-back-in-front-of-me game. It's more gratifying than dangling pieces of sauce-covered pasta over the edge of the high-chair tray, getting eye contact from everyone at the table, then opening the fist slowly and watching people scramble to catch the pasta before it hits the floor. It's almost better than throwing the precious pacifier into the rhinoceros exhibit at the zoo and watching a foolish, desperate and unraveled dad as he panicked and crawled over the railing and into the troubled waters to retrieve it. Because Daddy thought naptime would be unbearable without it. It's obvious who was in control!

I myself loved the youthful inquisitive phase of my kids asking droves of questions. It tests your broad-based knowledge and enhances your ability to comprehensively answer inquiries about things you have never previously given thought to or needed to explain before.

"Why is the moon always following me?"

"Why does my Play-Doh get hard?"

"Why do boys have nipples?"

"Why does it say 'One-size-fits-all'?"

"Why do I have that little red thing hanging down in the back of my throat?"

"Why is the bunny's color split down the middle? Did they cut two bunnies in half, one black and one white, and glue them together?"

"Why is one deer and more than one deer all called 'deer' instead of 'deers'?"

"Why aren't all twins born in June if 'Gemini' means 'twins'?"

"What happens if God forgets to feed Perky in guinea pig heaven?"

"Did you have us babies in your pouch?"

"How old will you be when you are no longer a young chick, Mommy?"

After most of the hardest questions had been answered then my offspring matured enough to make observations. Kids are so honest and frank that when they share their thoughts it is usually entertaining. However, many times they share them very loudly and in some very inappropriate situations. A mother learns the graceful art of dealing with public humiliation and the skills to quickly divert her youngster's attention to avoid further embarrassment.

Here are some good examples.

Once we were behind a very heavyset woman in the checkout line who was bending over to reach the cheese-cake and diet soda from underneath her cart. Her pants rode down and exposed more than necessary to Ryan who was right at eye level. He couldn't help but blurt out, "That big lady must be a plumber!" My face blended in with the bag of red apples in my arms, I gave him a glare of disapproval and tried to change the subject.

In the stall at a public family-style restroom Brad inquired, "Mommy, does your penis tingle too sometimes?"

Staring at a pregnant lady in the store, Nicole asked, "If you give birth upside down, would the baby come out your mouth?"

A confused older woman was trying on bras over her clothing in the department store which instantly caught my kids' attention. One asked me, "Isn't it called *underwear*, Mom?" Another one remarked, "Doesn't she know the dressing room isn't just for dresses?" The third one inquired, "What's the size of that one, Mommy?" Thank goodness her hearing wasn't too keen either. We swiftly changed directions and got the heck out of there.

As a little girl when my siblings were going to tickle me or wanted to wrestle, I would try to scare them off by saying, "I'm a fat girl and I can tough more bigger."

I leaned down to say good-bye and asked Nicole for a kiss. She inquired, "Do you want the French kind or the Eskimo kind?"

My friend was very tired driving home late one night. Her son said, "Mommy, how do you do that?" When she inquired what he was talking about he responded, "It's really cool that you can drive with your eyes closed like that." (By the way, they did make it home safe.)

During a discussion about his grandfather's funeral, Ryan stated, "Grandpa looked really mad to be dead!"

I received a call one day from Ryan's Boy Scout leader who was laughing and needed to share a story with me. He explained that at their holiday meeting some of the scouts were debating the validity of Santa Claus. Ryan, very concerned, cornered him and emphatically questioned, "Is Santa real or is it the parents who bring the presents? Come on, you *have* to tell me because when I grow up I'm going to have kids of my own, and I have to know if I'm the one who's supposed to bring the presents!"

One morning during a sprucing-up ritual, getting ready for school, Alex decided to try out his older brother's deodorant. As he headed out the door (to third grade mind you) he announced, "I put on armpit deodorant and I'm gettin' the ladies today!"

Brad was proud to show his drawing to his teacher. She looked puzzled as she studied the artwork that was a depiction of a green grassy field, and asked him what it was a picture of. He stated that it was wild horses running through a field. When she asked him why she didn't see any horses drawn in the picture he responded that they had run on to another field!

Alex wanted so badly to call a girl in his fourth-grade class of whom he was very fond. She was, in his words, "hot lava." Apparently little Miss Volcano made him nervous and she wasn't allowed to get calls from boys so Mr. Smooth, begged his older brother Brad to call her for him, and ask for a play date. (For fear of ending up in jail from asking a little ten-year-old girl over to play, Brad wisely declined. Good thinking, I say!)

I was at least thirty before I used a curse word in front of my mother, not wanting to offend her fragile ears, and I hope my offspring will refrain from spewing them as well. I'll admit to some occasional swearing (in private) which, like giving into a forbidden temptation, can be satisfying. But the aversion to some of those foul words was instilled in me long ago and still makes the little hairs in my inner ear smolder when I hear them.

A young child's long-awaited words can be priceless at times. Other times you wish you could keep your babies swaddled and pure and protected from the elements of life forever. Unfortunately, not even within these ultra-modern times could I have ever prepared myself for the shock I absorbed when my angelic daughter uttered these words in a meek and inquisitive tone: "Mommy, what does 'Get fu_ _ed' mean?" (Look, I can't even type it without blushing).

After my gasping stopped and my heart regained its normal beat the realization set in that it was mere innocence that provoked the curious question about some offensive and shameful public graffiti she had observed. Reluctantly, I spared my child some descriptive examples of just what that could mean or how she may experience it in her lifetime. It merely became a segue and began the next phase of upbringing and more valuable teachings. The "Just Say NO" campaign!

CHAPTER 13

Bliss-less Wives Club

I was busy bustling around the house, getting ready to go to my friend Chris's wedding. I brushed my daughter's hair while she teetered on the toilet seat; I held her steady with my knee against hers. I unknotted my son's urine-tainted shoelace with my teeth while giving my friend Coleen directions with the phone wedged between my left cheek and shoulder. Almost ready, I ran back upstairs to get a necklace off my dresser. When I entered my bedroom I caught sight of my husband, recently emerged from the bathroom with a towel tied around him, provocatively low. He stood in front of his wardrobe in the dimly lit closet looking puzzled. His left hand was rubbing his balding head while he rigorously scratched his butt like a ball-player. There's my Romeo!

He winked at me as if I should be turned on. I rolled my eyes at him in disbelief that he hadn't even dressed yet.

"What should *I* wear?" he moaned.

"What?" I responded in disbelief. I stood there perplexed for a moment.

"What should *I* wear?" he repeated in a bewildered tone.

"Are you kidding me?" I declared as I bounded into the closet.

We women have to decide if we are going to wear a dress, a skirt, a blouse, a shirt, dress suit, pants or a pantsuit. Then we have to decide whether we'll need a full slip, half-slip, stockings, nylons with a reinforced toe or pantyhose with the built-in panel, tights, and/or dress hose—and plan to have our undergarments match our outfit in case there is see-through, then adjust so there aren't unsightly panty lines or straps showing. We may need a strapless bra, one with padding or under-wires. Then we need the proper footwear: heels, flats, wedges, boots, platforms, open-toes or sandals. We have to decide on accessories, match our jewelry with our purse and our eye shadow with our shoes and coordinate our lipstick with our nail polish. After this whole ritual it's a wonder we still have energy left to go out. Then my husband has the audacity to ask,

"What should *I* wear?"

All these guys have to do is pick out a pair of pants and match it to their shirt for goodness sake! Can it be any easier than this? If they made dress suits in flannel he'd probably wear one all the time. I'll bet his retinas had become so camo-blinded that he couldn't see anything but blaze orange anymore. Maybe I'll have to put tags on his clothes. Then he could match a hammer tag and a nail tag, and there you have it! Or a drill and a drill bit for the more experienced fella. Ta-dah! Honey, I'm so proud of you for dressing yourself! And what an impressive bonus accomplishment that he actually decided whether to wear briefs, boxer shorts or a jewel pouch!

Anyway, somewhat exhausted, we got to the wedding just in the nick of time. The diaper bag was full to the brim, as if we were prepared to take a long trip. We poured into a pew. The young hopeful bride was ready to begin her journey up the aisle. Her starry eyes were filled with hope of bliss; she gleamed with infatuation. The event stirred the emotions of many.

The church was crowded. The single girls were gathered in the front pews crying and wishing it was their lucky day to become a promising new wife. All the married women were lined up in the back of the church sobbing and thinking, *That poor girl! Till death do you part! Even committing murder sometimes lets you off with less than a life sentence. Someone needs to stop her!* They tried to figure out a way to stall the wedding. *We could hold the sweet young thing up in the crying room until we talked some sense into her.*

I'll bet her response would probably be, *He's so nice!*

Puppies are nice too! Although they can also pee on your carpet if they have too much to drink, rub their genitals on your leg, sniff in embarrassing places and run away for a better treat down the street, then come back begging to be let back in. Sure, get a puppy. The advantage is that they at least can be put on a leash.

She would probably try to sway us by pointing out his attractiveness. *Don't get sucked in by his cuteness*, we tell her. *They are just one big scratch and sniff adventure!* Picture this: What if you come home tomorrow and you see a trail of dirty clothes from the front door all the way to the sofa. Following the stench of yesterday's chili (emitted from his gas) you find your prince sitting on the sofa in his thermal long-underwear with holes in the knees and stains down the front of his shirt from his Spaghetti-O lunch that dripped out of the can. His hair has only been combed with his hand since the day before. A six-pack of beer leans on his thigh. He clutches the remote to the television in one hand, crackers are lined up in front of him on the coffee table alongside the wad of chewing tobacco removed from his mouth and he holds a caulking gun loaded with Cheeze Wiz. Are you thinking his cuteness just wore off?

He's so different from all the other guys, she insists. Equally as disillusioned as we once were, we now endure the hemorrhoids, chronic headaches and stretch marks that marital bliss has caused us. Now we are members of the Bliss-less Wives Club. It's filled with droves of married women waiting for the happy ending. We know, like the persistent reminder of an impacted wisdom tooth, that most of us were conned into wedlock by false pretense. From generation to generation of hopeful female romantics, we bought into the optimistic notion, with confidence soaring, that we each found our man, the better treasure. Once the polish wiped away we found out we had been duped. In short, his cuteness *can* wear off.

By now we are sure he most likely will whine like a baby and expect his own, around-the-clock nursing staff to pamper his common cold. One can expect he will get sexually aroused by a glance, sound, smell, touch, or taste and want you to reciprocate to his whim in just about any location or position. Sometimes it consumes his thoughts. But usually, only momentarily! He will leave urine on the toilet seat and swear on a stack of Bibles that it wasn't him because he always puts the seat up. It is probable he will focus on money whether it is too much or too little. Chances are he will spend all kinds of time and attention on a sport or pastime instead of his family, causing jealousy and resentment that we have been replaced as his first love. Once the wedding tuxedo comes off, his desire to attract you with handsome attire will wane. He'll want to wear outdated flowered shirts or thermal ware. And he'll usually need our advice just to get to this level of appropriateness.

Finally, no matter how many children he fathers he will never do an even share of the work. Because we mothers are already nine months ahead in the amount of devotion and time spent nurturing, plus the relentless feat of pushing the rascals out during delivery puts him well behind with quite a bit of catching up to do.

Filled with persistent denial and conviction that she will make him the man she wants him to be, the bride marches on. Arriving at the altar ahead of her cue she beams at him, just to show us all that we don't know what we're talking about. Giving her the benefit-of-the-doubt is a female trait, so maybe she'll be one of the lucky ones to find the happiness that she's looking for. I wish them the best!

The wedding reception was filled with dancing, laughter and

expected drama. One of the bridesmaids, insisting that the dress is a one-size-fits-all, split her seam right down the side, exposing her mountains (overflowing from their cups) to every drunken male willing to help her with her dilemma. The divorced parents of the groom were having a tiff as to who was going to pay for the damages caused by the mysterious guest who rode his Harley into the hall. The bride's sister was having a cat-fight with the groom's sister because they were both planning on leaving with the good-looking D.J. See, that's where the trouble always begins. Listen to me! *Leave the D.J. and stop at the Humane Society on the way home to get a puppy!*

A wedding celebration often helps people rekindle their romantic feelings. Love can be contagious when you are surrounded by lovebirds (finely dressed and groomed specimens), alcohol and a free-spirited mood. We shared the anticipation of another couple joining the ranks, plodding through uncharted territory and pioneering their lives together.

On the ride home, my husband moaned about how much money he spent and that he thought the bartender stiffed him on his change while he was in the bar watching the game. Rubbing his neck with the palm of his hand, he complained that he thought he was catching a cold. Once at home he went straight to bed. I tucked in the kids and kissed them goodnight. I secured the house and I headed into the bathroom to begin my bedtime ritual.

I sat down on the toilet seat only to find it was wet and cold once again. Yep. His cuteness is long gone! My butt spotted with the recycled beer juice, I sighed with renewed disgust at the burden of perpetual potty training. How does this guy shoot a deer from a hundred yards away with exact precision to hit it in the heart? He can shoot a ball from half court and sink it through a rim that is only a few inches bigger than the ball itself. He just can't seem to get his little stream of bodily fluid, to go through an eighteen-inch seat, which he would braggingly want you to believe, is only inches away.

I quietly crawled into bed so not to disturb the flow of Casanova's grunting and snoring. The covers turned back revealed him adorned in his far from sexy fluorescent orange boxer shorts with the stretched-out waistband. It would appear he was on the prowl. He rolled over; his legs flopped apart like a puppy wanting his tummy scratched. Wiping some drool off his pillowcase he mumbled something about me smelling good. It was just the scent of soap used to wash the backs of my legs thanks to him. In the meantime I suggested he better get some sleep.

"It'll help your cold," I say, trying to distract him.

Whether he is frisky or flu-stricken, I'm in for one hell of a long night!

Just then the phone rang. Saved by the bell! I sprang from bed.

"I'll get it," I offered.

It is probably the newly wedded bride calling to borrow a stack of Bibles and to say she already wants to join our club!

CHAPTER 14
Three's a Crowd

One night I was unexpectedly jolted out of my sleep by my baby's bloodcurdling cries. I staggered to the nursery for the second time since bedtime. It seemed that all Bradley needed was a gentle back rub and the reassurance that I was only a screech away and that I'd successfully pass the drill in sufficient time.

Once my angel's wings were at rest and all was quiet again, I tip-toed back to my room to snuggle into my pillow-top mattress. With a glance at my clock radio and a quick calculation of the remaining slumber time, I silently pleaded for no further interruptions until daybreak. I tugged to regain my share of the blankets that my husband had conquered since I had left. I cast a slightly resentful glance as I noticed his peaceful and undisturbed look of contentment. I wished I could sleep through all of that noise.

As I settled in on my sliver of bed, he rolled over, passed gas and squinted at me with one eye like a pirate who's found the treasure. Amorous and frisky, he moved in close to see if I'd reciprocate. After spending half the day with my breasts hanging out and being groped by my newborn there is not an ounce of romance stirring inside my flannel pajamas.

I rolled toward the wall and knew if I lay real still, my lethargy would cause my matey to lose interest and (I hope) go away. His attention span was similar to a two-year-old's. I figured he'd forget about it and fall back to sleep but he left his dead-weighted arm, which felt like a Volkswagen, hanging over my side. It was either his way of cuddling or guarding the invaluable liquid gold inside his milkmaid treasure. Ahoy!

Startled again, my robotic body was in an upright position before I could comprehend what had awakened me. Since a couple of hours had passed since the last false alarm, it could have been a legitimate hunger cry. Baby and I trudged to the sofa in the family room for feeding time. It's usually a long process and I was thankful for the intermission between breasts.

It gave me an opportunity to wake Ryan, my five-year old, for school. He dressed while I packed his lunch and made his breakfast. Out of milk (from a carton, that is) I opted for the quick and simple solution, offering juice and peanut butter toast. We were running late. I urged him to speed up his dressing ritual. Multitasking, I burped Bradley on my shoulder while I loaded and organized Ryan's backpack. I wiped the stray spit-up off his knapsack with a handy dryer sheet (stuck to my pajama leg), which I doused with a quick spray of air freshener to disguise the odor—from sour milk to lilac scent.

I returned to the corner of the sofa to unveil my left milking contraption, held up in a nursing bra and concealed by a trap-door and silly circular pads (which, by the way, also work well in a pinch, under the legs of the pool table to level it out). Bradley, thus far the meekest member of the family, had recently figured out that the way to get seniority was to yell the loudest. He began to wail. Above his cries I heard the squeal of tires braking on the school bus as it rolled around the corner, ahead of schedule. The massive yellow motor vehicle stopped and opened its split doors (which would slap you in the face if you were standing too close) and the driver hunched forward and began to hurriedly honk the horn.

Ryan scrambled to jump into his shoes, and that's when I noticed his wildly mismatched socks. I made a quick assessment that it was only a minor crisis and chose not to focus on it. I carefully pushed up from the cushion and rose to my feet with the baby cradled in my arms, trying not to disturb his sucking rhythm. He clung to my nipple and my eyes watered with the pain. *Damn it!* I thought. Then through the streaked glass of the family room window I saw the bus pull away from our driveway.

My prodigy in disguise had peanut butter still stuck to the roof of his mouth and one sleeve of his jacket still hung empty as we kiss good-bye. With a gentle shove I suggested he have nothing less than a perfect day and reminded him to wipe the smudge of juice-covered peanut butter that clung to his upper lip. Grateful for cul-de-sac living, I knew the bus had to come back around for a second chance at picking up my youngster who was propelling himself down the driveway as he repeatedly tried to jab his arm into the mysterious sleeve. At least he was prepared with a mouthful of food that would last him the entire ride.

I returned to the window and give a final wave of encouragement. The bus pulled up to transport my little scholar. The elderly driver looked toward the house and enthusiastically waved back to me. With a grin on my face I returned the gesture. Little did he know that I had a suckling baby just below the window-sill (and probably the most voluptuous breasts he'd seen in years) just out of plain view. It could have been his best story at the company Christmas party!

The feeding came to an abrupt halt when Bradley turned from ravenous to rag doll. He was in a deep sleep and no amount of nudging or undressing would recapture his interest—similar to my husband after a satisfying sexual encounter. I guess they start their training early. Regaining my freedom, I unlatch him from my chest. I cautiously carried him to his crib for his morning nap.

Hoping that I might be able to sneak in a few winks before the next shift, I placed a pillow on one end of the sofa and grabbed the folded afghan that hung over the back of the rocking chair. Contentedly I snuggled the pillow and my frame quickly settled into the couch. Just then my sweet little three-year-old in her pink night-gown rounded the corner. She stood quietly, alternately lifting her bare feet on and off the cold linoleum floor. Her fist vigorously rubbed out the sleepiness in her right eye.

"Morning, Nicole," I greeted her. I refolded the afghan (that wasn't even warm yet) and returned it to the rocker. Funny, when I was young I hated taking naps but now I'd be ecstatic if I could get one. I proceeded to feed her, dress her and clean up the kitchen. We played quietly for a bit. Before I knew it my kindergartener would be home from school, scurrying up the driveway dragging his jacket in one hand by the still-mysterious sleeve. He tumbled his lilac-scented backpack in the door to announce his arrival. Evidently, he didn't get his daily allowable portion of non-toxic paste at school that day nor was he resourceful enough to suck the peanut butter off his sleeve that he wiped there earlier that morning, so he was hungry.

There were only nine and a half months left until summer vacation. I can't imagine why much of it was a blur! I had flashbacks of how much simpler having two children used to be. Two's company, three's a crowd! I don't mean to refer to the term "crowd" as a negative connotation. Usually, I think the more the merrier. But there is no doubt about it, the third child does create a huge parenting challenge and definitely has heightened all five of my senses.

Sight: The eyes in the back of my head formed as quickly as the afterbirth was shed by my body on the delivery table. It is inevitable and a valuable lifesaver. Nursing a baby requires great commitment, patience and time. Those first-born are usually very calm and contented because we have more time to create a peaceful atmosphere for them.

When Ryan was a baby, during feeding time he would look up at me with his little adoring face and we would share a tender loving smile. But by the time my third child came along, the mood was altered. Brad looked up at me with one beady little eye like that of the salmon on a hors d'oeuvre' table. He quickly slurped each ounce of his meal as if anticipating an interruption. He often rolled his eyes back trying to see what the commotion was going on behind him. I would try to stay calm and collected while policing the other well-nourished children who would try to take advantage of Mom when she was in a compromised position.

Of course, the one permanent marker I didn't put away was the one Nicole's long fingers could retrieve from under the refrigerator. She began to practice abstract design on the wall. I sensed Ryan in the next room, somehow knowing that he'd found a morsel of charred wood left on the hearth from the previous night's fire. I tried to get to it before he could dabble with it as if it were sidewalk chalk, only it caused indelible markings etched on all that he touched, such as his clothing, hands, carpet, etc. I was too late!

In situations like these I gave Bradley a quick improvised smile to let him know that everything was fine. I struggled to keep my tone calm and yet be persuasive enough to get my little rascals to curtail their activities. Poor little guy. (He'll probably be a contender in eating contests in the future, since he's been taught how to literally eat on the run.) In time, I learned to corral both of the bigger kids in the same room with us to deter mischief and sometimes I even stood while nursing the baby so I was up on my feet, and ready for action.

Smell: It has taken many little handpicked bouquets of dandelions delivered to my front door to help wipe away the memory of the time when all three of my kidlings had the stomach flu. They each had equally vile and disgusting substances projecting from opposite ends of their bodies which created an indescribable and almost unforgettable scent. Every mother knows there isn't enough lilac spray….

Hearing: Listening to multiple sources with each individual ear was mastered early on. I could hear a recital of Ryan's new song that he learned at school, nodding and praising him the whole way through endless verses while my other ear-drum simultaneously absorbed Nicole's diagnosis of our cat Gus' rare sickness along with her projected treatment and recovery plan for him.

Two ears work just fine. It's when the third child throws his story into the mix. So when I heard some mumbling about the stupid bus driver yelling at Brad and that he and his friend might not be able to ride the bus anymore, that's when I noticed I was having a hearing problem.

"Wait! What? Hold it, one at a time. Gus' disease is called what? Can you hum the eighth verse that sounds just like the first while I find out about how and why your brother braided a girl's hair to *what*?"

Taste: Rarely do I taste my children. Although a series of sloppy good-night kisses or haphazard and wet good-bye kisses does come to mind. The kind when my toddlers lacked pucker technique and just basically held their drool-covered mouths open so we could bump our lips together and call it a kiss. But this mommy can never get too many kisses and with two cheeks and a set of lips I am well equipped to handle three kids, all at the same time!

There was the time that my kids prepared me a chocolate cake with imaginary frosting from the Easy Bake oven and cooked me spaghetti by soaking the noodles in really hot water for a long time in one of their slightly rinsed sand toys and invited me to a Mother's Day lunch. That was a taste that was both memorable and breathtaking!

Touch: Two hands are amazingly adequate amongst multiple children—most of the time. I can wipe up one spill while dishing out food to another. I can give a congratulatory pat on the back to one child while scolding and shaking my index finger at another. I can put bait on one hook while taking a fish off another. Having two sides on my body allows my children, one on either side, to nestle under my arms to hear a bedtime story; I can keep one balanced on each leg, held tightly for a lecture. Two arms can carry two offspring through the pouring rain. Two feet, one child per foot, can carry and shuffle two dancers to a waltz.

The third child is worth every bit of panting, blowing and swollen ankles. He becomes the tie-breaker. She creates the opportunity for a driver, spotter and skier. He helps to diversify eenie, meenie, minee, mo. She becomes the third ring to complete the circus (with me as the ringleader). I wouldn't trade any of them for the pot of gold at the end of the rainbow. But the triplicate offspring does compel parents to adapt to the challenge of uneven proportions.

I invested in a lot of extra protection—lilac scented air freshener and I suggest you do the same. It can transform and disguise *almost* any foul smell.

CHAPTER 15

Up North?

There is brief excitement at the first snowfall of winter. I anxiously inspect footprints left by the mysterious wildlife with whom I share my domain. They seem to exist primarily during nocturnal hours. One day I hope to catch a close-up glimpse of the mighty deer scampering through our yard or eating from the feeder only fifteen feet out our back door. For me that would be enough excitement. But for many men in the northwest, they long for a closer, grander encounter.

Having grown up in a family of hunters I am all too familiar with the tradition of deer hunting. My dad, a skilled marksman and avid hunter, has been delivering a slab of venison each and every year as long as I can remember. He thought it was good clean fun. Up early to hunt, then home to hit the hay after hiking in nature all day. Upon his return my gracious mother always looked pleased and showered my dad with congratulatory praise of his kill….until he returned to the garage to unpack the rest of his gear. Then, under her breath, she groaned, looking at the venison and no doubt thinking, *What the hell am I going to do with this thing now?* (Though she never let on that she was less than enthused.)

To my father, outwitting the massive buck of the woods was a masculine hobby requiring great cunning skill, patience, accuracy and perseverance. My mother felt that supporting him in this hobby required the same attributes. It was her wifely duty to excel in creative culinary arts that would transform a tough, chewy, worthless hunk of meat into a delectable meal fit for a king, all the while leaving him believing she enjoyed the whole experience. In other words, outwitting the massive buck of the house.

To me, growing up watching the whole drama, it seemed very silly. As a girl, I shared an enthusiasm for guns. I know hunting can be as much of a female sport as it is for males. I liked shooting and all of the trappings except for one minor detail. I didn't like killing animals and didn't like it that others did it for sport. Each season, I would debate every convincing argument I had in me to keep my dad from tagging another buck. But he claimed it was his duty to help thin the herd and rode off into the woods with his boots covered in doe urine. And there we were waiting with cleavers in hand upon his return, praising him and butchering the thing on the kitchen table like primitive savages. Can't we just go to the store and buy our meat wrapped in cellophane like everyone else?

For some avid hunters like my father, hunting season starts well before November. Many go after small game like birds, rabbits and squirrel. It was always an adventure poking around in the freezer section at our house. We had turkey, duck, pheasant, mallards, ring-neck, grouse and partridge with all but the pear tree. They were odd shapes, frozen in all sorts of contortionist positions. My favorite was the rabbit in mid-stride. Not to eat, just to play tricks on people with. Other friends had a Barbie car. My Barbie rode in style on top of the rabbit. I claimed it got better gas mileage. Once I freaked out my science teacher really good with "Bugs." And there was the one year my brother put on a magic show and the audience was aghast when he pulled that gross rabbit out of a hat. The poor thing was in a freezer-burn state for years. I think Mom was stumped with that one. No one ever requested hasenpfeffer, so she kept quiet, hoping that jackrabbit would be forgotten. Apparently I am the only one who remembered it was still there.

I guess it was inevitable that my husband too would be a hunter. Though his modern-day hunt played out a bit differently. First, he would tell me about some bad news he had: he was going up north to go deer hunting. To me, it was hardly bad news. A few days without him around would be like a vacation. I mumbled some "I'll miss you" boloney that I hoped sounded sincere.

"Where are you going?" I inquired.

"I can't remember, somewhere up north," would be his annoyed response.

Never before was such a vague answer quite so inadequate! *Up north? Are you kiddin' me?* That could mean just about anywhere between our house in Wisconsin, and Rudolf's place in the North Pole for cripe sake.

"Who's all going?" I asked curiously.

"Some of the guys," he responded lacking any information whatsoever.

"When do you think you'll be back?" I questioned.

"When I hunt down a nice big trophy buck I'm proud of and good enough to mount," he insisted.

I decided to hold my tongue instead of complaining about what a double standard it is that he goes off, without a care, into the wilderness and doesn't think twice or look back once. Someday I'm going to do it and see how he likes it.

Hunting is such an elaborate sport. You can't tell me men don't love to shop! There is so much specialized gear, decoys, guns, ammunition, calls, waders, clothing and accessories. If men only put that much energy into sprucing up for their wives I bet there would be many happier couples these days. If women believed all they had to do was to pee on their husband's shoes to get some authentic attention, they might be willing to stoop that low. Nah! On second thought he pees on his shoes enough for the both of us.

I'll just let him go and enjoy the peace and quiet while he's gone.

The days prior to his departure I laundered every article of blaze orange he owned. I lovingly cooked pots of chili, an elaborately decorated cake showing a buck in the woods in five colors of icing, a pan of corn-bread and a vegetable medley. While he went to bed early, I stayed up extra late waiting for the cinnamon swirl muffins to come out of the oven and cool so he could take them with him on his journey to the northern hemisphere, in the early morning hours. I rose early to see that he had all the essentials he needed: warm socks, doe urine, luck, hand warmers, well wishes, ammunition, etc...

A few hours later I was taking the kids out to run errands. As we drove up our main road I caught a glimpse of my favorite green kettle in the ditch. Puzzled, I slowed down and saw my baking pan and brown casserole dish on the shoulder. Angrily I retrieved my dishes (with the contents still lukewarm) while my confused children watched me through the steamed-up car windows. Scattered amidst the discarded buffet I also found many empty beer cartons alongside the road. One could only assume there wasn't room in the cooler for them both, *my* stuff and the beer! I see which one was the priority. A bunch of drunken men, staggering around a field somewhere with loaded guns in their hands...It's a brilliant pastime. Maybe there should be locking devices on triggers until its owner passes a Breathalyzer?

Now my husband insisted earlier in the week that he had all the remaining food taken care of. By the trail of empty wrappers and receipts I could see he attempted to include the five food groups. Cheese (curls), fruit (filled danish), beef (jerky), veggie (pizza), beer (light brand which he claims is mostly water) and cigars (for dessert).

Despite my unwelcome discovery on the side of the road, the extended weekend was a delight. My kids and I had such relaxing fun, with little care as to the time. We came and went and ate when we were hungry. Soon our fiesta weekend drew to an end as Sunday evening approached.

In came the big hunter. He reeked of cigars, stale beer and beef jerky. The cooler was empty and so were the matchbook covers from Candy's Cookie Jar Bar, and only a few leftover single dollar bills. A classy establishment, I'm sure. Unfortunately, the truck bed was filled with plenty of dirty laundry and a big old buck.

The poor, beautiful animal, who was abruptly and violently taken from his family, hung in our garage. His bright red rubbery tongue dangled out the side of his mouth and scared the children. My kids and the deer, stared at each other in awe.

"I went out to hunt for your dinner like in the pioneer days," my husband boasted.

"Mommy did too, Daddy. She went out and found it alongside the road! We didn't have to go way up north to get it. It was so good. It was already made and everything. It was amazing!" the kids proudly responded.

He looked up immediately, his eyes like a deer's caught in headlights. I should have used the Chevy on him just then, but it was more fun watching him squirm.

Before long, I too was gifted with a venison carcass. We decided to forgo the butchering ourselves so I could have more time to wallow in venison recipes. Pretending I loved the challenge, Betty Crocker and I were on a mission to wow him and his friends. Besides their great drinking stories (guess you had to be there) about their drunken foolishness, a good venison dish gives a hunter true bragging rights.

"Here, you've got to try this, it's the best you've ever tasted!" he would badger our guests.

Next, he wanted to have the buck (which he nicknamed "Big-Daddy-O") decapitated, stuffed and mounted on the wall above our bed. He tried every convincing argument he could come up with. He thought I could use the antlers as a jewelry or a candle holder. He could hang his hat on it. He even suggested the antlers could be a handle to aid me in various positions during arousal time. But I'm absolutely sure there will be no sexual excitement anytime soon if I have to share my room with *two* empty headed Big Daddy-Os.

A couple weeks had passed and I thought I deserved at least one night out with some friends. My husband didn't really like the idea.

"Where are you going?" he asked irritably.

I shrugged. "I can't remember, somewhere up north."

"Who's all going?" Curiously he demanded.

"Some of the guys," I offered back.

"When do you think you'll be back?" he questioned.

"When I hunt down a nice big trophy buck I'm proud of and good enough to mount," I responded.

"Do you have any singles on you? We're going to see Peter Piper and his Pickled Pepper Dance Revue. You and Big Daddy-O shouldn't wait up."

He stood there stunned as I cheerfully closed the door behind me. My girlfriends Cheri, Lila, Maryann, Karen and I laughed about it during dinner that night at a local restaurant, knowing he was home steaming mad. On the way home I stopped at my mom's to visit and pick up a few things, trying to stall and stay out late.

The next day, I got up refreshed and felt like cooking. Abracadabra! I made him a delicious dish from a fourteen-year-old, freezer-burned rabbit and called it venison stew. He claimed it was the best he ever had and called all his friends to brag, urging them to come and try it. It was just getting too easy to outwit Big Daddy-O! No matter how silly they are, supporting our men is what we do best. You taught me well, Mom!

CHAPTER 16

The Term "Good Morning" Is an Oxymoron!

Awakened by D.J. madness, I realize how urgently my presence is needed downstairs as a rhythmical pattern beats a familiar tune. I hear the cupboard, pantry and refrigerator doors opening and banging shut at even intervals. If there is no intervention, the refrain to follow will be snap, crackle and pop! Snap—as the stacked plastic bowls bounce off the counter. Crackle—the sound of cereal being multiplied by the bottoms of little feet. And a finale of Pop— as the cover is launched off the milk jug as it plunges to the floor, causing an abrupt volcano of 1% milk on my linoleum.

The term "Good morning" is a pleasant thought in theory but I find it to be more of an oxymoron. I can do mornings just fine; I just wish they started a little slower and later, especially on weekends.

This particular day I am blessed by Ryan's indecisiveness, which I swear is usually a curse! After he poured half of the contents of the cereal into a small pile on the table he decided he doesn't like the prize in the bottom of the box. He is now trying to shovel the crispy morsels back into the receptacle with some reluctant kernels stuck to his sweaty palms. Not bad—he got about two-thirds of them back in, leaving only about 1,764 pieces strewn about. As he chases them aimlessly about the floor with the broom, I wipe off the table and chairs.

"Let's have some Mickey Mouse pancakes," I suggest with newfound enthusiasm.

As the pancakes heat up, Nicole stands on a chair and leans

over to peer into the pan with anticipation. She just can't help herself and drizzles extra batter into the pan, giving some of our Mickey's three ears; one even looks to be smoking a cigar. Brad's empty digestive system prances to the sporadic moves of a four year old wasting precious time. He dances and sings a silly little ditty to kill time. I'm going to try that dance the next time I'm in the doctor's waiting room to see if it helps get the staff to hurry me through.

Finally we are happily munching our pancakes. Then someone spills an unclaimed glass of juice while my back is turned cutting Bradley's pancakes into cubes. The juice runs toward the lowest leg on the table and splatters over the edge to the floor. The pulpy juice bloats up the remaining crumbs left behind by the sweeper. An oxymoron, I tell you.

After the kitchen cleanup, it's time to really start our day. Could our horoscopes have predicted such a hectic beginning to our day? It can only get better from here, right? As long as Ryan doesn't delve into any major investments, Nicole avoids getting involved with a Sagittarian male and Bradley doesn't choke on the mouse's ears, they should be okay. As for me, I could use a wealthy Sagittarian male who will feed me pancakes. Sounds like the man of my dreams. I just hope Mr. Right knows how to do the Heimlich maneuver!

In the spirit of Christmas I thought it would be great to start a new holiday tradition with my kids this year. I am taking them out into my parents' woods where we'll cut down our own, live Christmas tree. I'd like a beautiful, shapely and full, eight-foot-tall tree with medium needle length. It's tough to get me to deviate from my plan once my untamed enthusiasm gets rolling like an avalanche. So despite the thermometer reading zero degrees we bundle up and get ready to go.

Wait! Can that be right? We turned the darn thing from side to side and upside down. Sure enough! It still reads zero! "We'll be fine," I say reassuringly. "We're not going to be out there that long."

We trudge through the deep snow, down to the woods. Bradley tired quickly and plopped down on the toboggan I was pulling. Soon after pretending to help push, Nicole is resting most of her weight on the sled as well. I'm getting quite a workout. The sun is out which makes it feel much warmer than it really is, but the air bites at any exposed skin nonetheless.

Once inside the woods, shielded from the wind, all three kids scamper in opposite directions. Finding the right tree is impossible. The humanitarian begs to bring home the Charlie Brown tree like it's a new-found puppy. The ax murderer who is getting a first try at using a weapon swings with vigor, attempting to cut down everything in sight so we can have a tree in every room of the house. We all keep our distance. The meanderer is wandering off, following an intriguing trail of bunny droppings with little care or recollection of why we were here in the first place.

How could this be so difficult? I'm not very picky. Just a nice, simple Christmas tree between three and ten feet tall will do just fine. Long or short needle is okay. With this vast selection of evergreens I thought it would be so easy to find a shapely fir, balsam or blue spruce. We roamed like Alice in Wonderland searching for some normalcy. Most of the trees were deformed—not something you'd display in a tree stand in the center of your living space and feel awed by its beauty. We knew we'd passed up some better ones but by now we were too frigid to go back. The colder we got the less discriminating we became.

Puffing through our steaming scarves with only our eyes showing, Ryan and I dragged the heavy toboggan. On it were two extremely cold, tired, sniffling children complaining of snow in their boots, wet gloves and cold ears; and yes, a resemblance of a tree. It met the description of a tree anyway. It was an evergreen, with a trunk and branches. Boy, did we want to get home! And thank goodness all the lumberjacks still had their limbs intact.

"This one will be just fine," I rally us as we load it into our vehicle.

On the way home I talked about Christmas time and being happy with what we have. Not being greedy. Some of the greatest treasures are free. Giving of yourselves and sharing your time together is better than expensive gifts. I could hardly stop at Stein's Garden Center on the way home to buy a perfect, fake tree, now could I?

We erected our horticultural find in the stand after the ax murderer helped to chop inches of wood away to taper the trunk. In the warmth of the house its full, soft branches spread out. It was as huge around as it was tall but it kept tipping over, due to its disproportionate size. Our supply of decorations seemed sparse as my humanitarian tried to disburse them evenly on the spindly limbs. My meanderer pulled things from pockets, an eclectic array of treasures that had been found in the woods, and added them to the twig branches. All but the rabbit pellets which I insisted should be left outside. But damn it, we are going to feel proud of our ridiculous tree. We gaze at it until nightfall. Christmas bush, O Christmas bush!

As I lay motionless on a mattress oozing with money, a gorgeous, buff man leans down to me and gently lifts my head and puts his face close to mine. He is wearing little draped around his midsection but has a sign around his neck that reads: **Sagittarius.** There is a wonderful scent of pancakes in the distance and a muffled tune, "It's a Small World," dances in my head. As his sweet gentle lips touch mine I am awakened by an alarming commotion downstairs. I scurry to throw on my robe and head down the hallway toward the crisis. Please tell me *this* is the part that is the dream!

As I get closer I hear a familiar refrain of snap, crackle and pop! Snap—as the top half of the bush bends over and breaks in two from the weight of Gus, our curious cat who climbed to the top. Crackle—the sound that dozens of fragile ornaments make as they splat and shatter on the floor. And the finale of Pop—as the star is launched off the top and the tree yanks out of its stand, spilling murky green spruce juice which will permanently adhere to the backing in my carpet.

I stand there thinking, once again, that the term "Good morning" is a pleasant notion in theory. I tell you, I think it's an oxymoron! And with all the spirit of Christmas, it can only be followed with "Have a great day"!

CHAPTER 17

Divorce: Finally the Cat's Out of the Bag

A good acronym for "divorce" would be: Deserving Independence, Vital, Overwhelmingly Rejuvenating, Colonoscopy Experience! In short—a healthy cleansing of the toxic and unnecessary $#*! out of your life! (My mom just gasped.)

There are a myriad of reasons why many in the baby boomer generation were destined to fail the "till death do you part" portion of our wedding vows. Maybe it was because women with their new-age smoldering bras were getting tired of the adage that behind every successful man was a terrific woman. This was absolutely the truth and yet many (successful men) were the only ones who couldn't see the smoke signals or admit it was true. She was the one who was scrubbing the floors he walked on, feeding his belly and ego, pressing his clothes and sending him into the world with stylish attire and bolstering him with confidence that he could accomplish anything. Just like our mamas taught us to do. But Mom, he isn't in kindergarten anymore!

After many centuries of complete devotion to serving our masterful leaders, our patience with slavery wore thin as the realization dawned on us that it usually was an extremely capable woman, bearing much of the beauty and brains of the couple, who was smoothly running most of the household and keeping its contents intact. So it was inevitable that we would come to believe our partners owed us far more than just a place to stay. We wanted appreciation for our wit, wisdom and warm meals. The obedient wife and silent children were no longer trophies to be paraded around like an old classic Corvette, or possessions of equal value to his beer can collection. Many men took advantage of their positions, behaved inappropriately and were far too content to realize there might be consequences to their actions and that the throne they put themselves on could crumble. The result was a long overdue mutiny. Long live the queen!

There was a time when the man was the main breadwinner and the woman took care of the domestic chores. He would hold out a stack of cash and she would hold out a stack of clean shirts and they would swap on the count of three. Why would women choose to continue taking care of most of the operations of the home, the children and themselves while many ladies were working alternate jobs or professions and bringing home their own loaves of bread? And even still felt guilty when the meatloaf crumbled or the blackened chicken was a little too charred due to an extra-long teacher's conference or emergency toilet plunging.

Superwomen were exhausted from running the show with little help or recognition. They began to question why they really needed the extra baggage and disappointment he provided. Finally, when he couldn't keep up his end of the bargain in the bedroom without a strong dose of Viagra, well, it was a done deal! We started to raise our standards as to what we thought our husbands were supposed to be fulfilling in the arrangement. Many of them came up way too short. Or they proved to have had more flaws than could be feasibly corrected in a lifetime and we would die trying! In translation: Until death do *I* part!

Sometimes admitting defeat is easier than conquering something not worth fighting for. Like the time that my solution to getting my drunken sweetheart to listen to me was to send a plate of hot Hungarian goulash whizzing past his head and explode on the wall. It splattered on the surrounding furniture, carpet and curtains with a few straggling, saucy noodles landing in his hair.

Even if a fork pierced his forehead he would still have been oblivious to the explosion around him. Needless to say he was not helpful in the cleanup either. So I learned two valuable lessons. Liquids are more successful in getting someone's attention. The other was to invest in a Shop Vac.

When I felt my marriage was spiraling out of control, my disappointment ran deep. The most hopeful resolution I could imagine was that I'd get a feline companion to replace the man I originally married. He would be that easy to replace. I always wanted a house cat but he wouldn't allow it because he had allergies. Each attorney visit got me one step closer to the gentle, loveable companion I longed for. He would come when I call, cuddle affectionately, would keep himself clean without reminders, didn't need three meals a day and would never leave urine on the toilet seat.

We tend to get spiteful when our partner doesn't provide adequate care or fulfill their expected role. They may even embarrass and humiliate us. Their once-cute habits come to grind away at our subconscious—like the putrid smell of chewing tobacco and the already annoying gestures and jokes. These behaviors become as intolerable as repeated drunkeness or violent and abusive actions. Or the overwhelming betrayal of trust when one discovers perversions and hidden cameras in the master bedroom. Some men allow money, alcohol, violence and alternate substances to dictate who they are or use them as a scapegoat to justify and pump up their egos. We say: *Sorry fellas, it didn't help. It just compounded the problem and made you even bigger jerks and losers than we ever could have imagined.* And even in a no-fault divorce court, it's glaringly obvious who was at fault anyway!

Only minimal satisfaction can come from rearranging the furniture and waiting up late to hear your drunken partner stagger in and stub his toe on the sofa. A little more satisfaction can be gained by slipping laxatives in his morning coffee and implying the consequence must be due to overindulging behavior the night before. Scaring a cheating husband by putting poison ivy in his boxers would be no more of a solution than sending an obsessed man naked pictures of his own mother to deter him from scouring up all the porn he can find. These men may still seek out forbidden pleasures. And finally, love isn't meant to hurt, intimidate or scare. If the brute has the fire of the devil in his eyes, run! Violence to women and especially toward children just shouldn't be tolerated and the door should hit the ass, on the way out!

The most satisfaction we'll gain is to cut our losses and to move on to better, more positive things. We deserve to be happy, but on our own terms. It's about time we put our foot down and show our kids how a lady should be treated. For me, ripping apart my wedding dress with my teeth was some of the best foreplay I've had in years. Hauling my ex-husband's pile of crap belongings out of my house was the best therapy I could have asked for. And burning our wedding photo album caused a chimney fire that introduced me to fourteen eligible firemen. Fate does work in mysterious ways!

Whenever your previous spouse comes around, be sure to flaunt the power tools and chain saw you got custody of, then ride around and wave good-bye to him on the lawn *and* tractor that he always wanted, and you now own. Inquire about the crochet-topped hand towels, incomplete glass set, broken toaster and ugly plaid sofa he got as equalization or parting gifts, so as not to seem insensitive. It only seems fair he should receive as an added bonus to the divorce acknowledgement the collection of sleazy lingerie he purchased for his bride that never provoked an adequate performance out of him regardless of the discomfort she withstood wearing it. Also the discovered secret bedroom videos laden with his partner's lasting looks of disgust and her perpetual expressions of disappointment.

The godsend for me is that I believe I gave it my all and did whatever I could to save both of my marriages. Yes. I said both. I am a slow learner. I have so many ex-husbands I have to number them. I'm not proud of that but I gave both of them the opportunity to fix and correct their serious problems and they both refused. I find peace knowing that I didn't fail my marriages, my marriages failed me. I have stopped beating myself up over it. In fact it allows me two more (ex-anniversary) days of the year I can eat celebratory cake without guilt. Along with a glass of milk that is "half full"!

It's important to realize you can't change things that are out of your control, but that you do have the option to get out of a bad situation and move on to a better life. It can be a much healthier and happier existence in the long run. And trust me, if there are children in the picture, kids are very perceptive as to what is dysfunctional. You would be doing them a favor by not staying.

It's like bringing home a pretty red turtleneck sweater that looked so darling that we fell for in the store, from false advertising or misrepresentation. Then we get it home and in time it doesn't fit right or squeezes too tight around the neck. We all have to face the fact that we make horrible mistakes at times. That shouldn't mean we should be forced to wear something that makes us extremely uncomfortable or is totally a wrong fit for the remainder of our lives as a punishment. Unfortunately there is a no-money-back guarantee and will probably cost you a lot to return.

A prayer I embrace:

God grant me Serenity, to accept the things I cannot change
Courage, to change the things I can
Wisdom, to know the difference
And bravery, knowing when to get out!

If we teach our kids as to what is fair and right, equality will come. But the best revenge is to raise our sons to grow up to be far better men than their fathers could ever be. The shame that these fathers will feel should catapult them into becoming the men they were expected to be in the first place. For some men there is little hope. I say leave those cases for other women to try to tame. Since it would appear all of us divorcees are swapping partners, one at a time.

It is true there are some bad female apples that have tainted our species too. Women are not perfect and I do admit this is a slanted presentation about the downfalls of men. But it's precisely because I have a female perspective of what I and others have experienced. In all fairness, though, for those women who are giving us girls a bad name, shame on you. Be nice, be fair, but fight for your rights in a dignified manner!

I admire the decent men who have evolved into the equality of the new-age marriage. They respect their wives for the true partners they are. I am a hopeful romantic and I am confident there are some good guys left out there, and one of them is for me. I am determined to get it right (my horoscope claims the third time is the charm). It's a glorified rummage sale and we may have to dig through many piles (of men) to find a keeper. If you're lucky enough to find a good one, be sure to hang onto him. Or keep searching to find the right fish in the sea or the red sweater that was meant for you. He should make you feel safe, warm and comfortable. He will compliment, support and accentuate the best in you. In return you will gently care for him and occasionally lay flat and reshape if necessary.

Respect is to be earned, not given. Beware of the intoxicated guys with noodles in their hair and a fork in their forehead. Or the crazy ones who have the look of the devil in their eyes and are holding a box of used lingerie and tragic home sex tapes. Altering those guys may prove to be an insurmountable and unworthy task. Life is too short!

Ahhh! My therapist was right. I feel so much better now!

Live well, laugh often and love much!!

CHAPTER 18

Rival Survival

I was born in an era when it was convenient to have all of us kids doing the same thing and acting alike. According to my dad we should be seen and not heard. (It was a great theory but unfortunately for him, I'm just not the type who can stay quiet.) We dressed alike, wearing hand-me-downs until they didn't have a shred of play left in them, and we had to share everything—except underwear and gender-specific toys, of course! You wouldn't dare cross your blues with pinks back in the day.

My mom even thought it was easier and more efficient to have all of us get sick at the same time, nurse us all back to health at once and then be done with it. When my sister Sandy got pinkeye we all shared the same wash cloth. When my brother Brian got the stomach flu we all had to go in the bedroom to play with him and share in his misery until we all were feverish and nauseously embraced a plastic pail in our laps too. When my brother Connor got a sore throat and needed a tonsillectomy we all had to eat off the same spoon and line up at the doctor's office. So when we found out I needed major back surgery my siblings were a wreck with worry because they thought my parents were going to knock them down the stairs or run them over with the car so we would all share that experience too. Luckily for them, Mom and Dad could only afford one major surgery and I happened to be the lucky contestant.

I can't say I shared the same mentality when I became a mother. Times had changed. No more freewheeling. No way would any kid who forgot his hat be allowed to pick somebody else's out of the lost and found and return it the following day for the next forgetful recipient. And the idea that the same comb, straightened the hair of each member of the whole third grade class on picture day—these days, that would be grounds for disciplinary measures. Nowadays, during a louse outbreak some schools use scare tactics; each student gets his hair searched while all the other kids sit by watching and dreading their turn. The kids who had been cleared break out into a raucous refrain of "Bad boys, bad boys, whatcha gonna do, whatcha gonna do when they come for you?" Yes, times have changed and I hope none of my children get a pink slip.

Despite all the precautions I used, I wasn't lucky with the chickenpox. Three of my kids each got it consecutively, one week at a time. Quarantine had failed. I pleaded with my employer that I needed time off of work to care for my sickly children. This was hardly the way I envisioned using my vacation days. Instead of me in a hot tub, sipping champagne with a good-looking man, I spent three long weeks nurturing my leopard-spotted youth. It entailed bathing them in oatmeal, lathering calamine lotion on each polka dot, making fun lunches, distracting their attention away from the insatiable urge to itch and assuring each of them that if they picked at the scab they would get a scar for life. Once again, nobody listened to Mom. Each of my kids has a permanent pox scar on his or her face as proof, my perpetual opportunity to silently remind them, for the rest of their lives, that they should have listened to their mother!

As a parent, I preferred to challenge the gender guidelines. We defied the laws of color that divided us in a previous world of pink and blue. It was a free-for-all in our house. The Easy Bake oven was as universal as power tools. Much beyond their dad's comfort level, I encouraged all my sons to clutch dolls (boy dolls, of course) around the house with them and my daughter to dabble with model cars.

No matter what era, though, getting kids to get along is another ongoing challenge. I don't care how many children you have or what their gender is; they will always find some idiosyncrasy that they can use as a tool to irritate their siblings with. Whether it's a weird tic, annoying sound, contorted facial expression or bodily noise, they quickly learn how to prey on each other's weaknesses. Fortunately as adults we can ignore most of the petty squabbles and gestures especially when they occur in the privacy of our own homes. But when their worst behaviors are displayed in the checkout line or during a solemn ceremony it tempts us to question, "*Why did I think having children would be fun?*" And that is only the mild stage.

Next comes the snatching away of cherished toys from one another or hiding the other's favorite stuffed doggie or life-support blankie merely to cause a commotion. And heaven forbid anyone yank the Nuk away from the toddler's lips just to hear him wail. Kids know how to heighten the discord in any room by manipulating each other. It usually is not learned, it is an instinctive default that causes youngsters to test the waters, learn how to use their power for leverage in the pecking order. But most important it is a huge test for parents to learn patience and tolerance, and don't forget about unconditional love!

The older they get, the more creative their methods. Jumping out of a dark place or from a hidden spot is very popular. They learn quickly that a mother's shriek is priceless and a sibling's frightened tears are hysterical. They find humor in hiding while you frantically search every last imaginable spot for them when you think they are lost. Children become giddy beyond recognition when they scribble permanent-marker mustaches and bushy Groucho Marx eye-brows on their sleeping siblings as a reward for being the first one to fall asleep. Little stinkers find amusement when they hold the door to the bathroom shut and watch the nervous dance of their sister's fragile bladder outside pleading for entry.

Sometimes their teasing is more subtle and unplanned. When my daughter tripped in her ill-fitting Halloween costume and fell to the ground, she lay there kicking and screaming for help. Her flailing arms and legs stuck out of the sides and bottom of the large box around her, which was painted like a die. Knowing she couldn't get up, her brothers taunted her, threatening to take her candy which was dumped on the ground in front of her, close enough to smell. She cried as I called off the bullies and came to her rescue. I carefully got her back on her feet and helped her gather her valuable treats (receiving by way of thanks two Reese's Peanut Butter Cups and a Tootsie Roll).

Sometimes kids' pranks are more deliberate. Once when I was little, my brother thought it would be funny to mess with my favorite Cheerful Tearful doll. She was supposed to be filled with water so that when you put her arm in the downward position she would let out a sweet little cry and shed tears. I was devastated when he put water in her tear ducts, so that when you put her arm down she would pee in her pants! The only satisfaction I got was when Mom put her arm in a downward position and spanked his butt and he cried hard. Momentarily I was cheerful, that he was tearful! But neither I nor my doll ever fully recovered from the trauma of that day.

The older kids get, the more that can be at stake. Among my sons, there is the occasional jockeying for the same girl's affection. One son flirts just as an ego booster to see if he can gain his brother's girlfriend's attention while loving to watch his younger sibling curdle with furious envy. They would never cross the invisible line in the sand with one another but surely do butt heads and lock horns right up to the line at times.

Occasionally, there are the mischievous pranks they pull on each other, like one of them secretly planting Tabasco sauce (or a pill to enhance a bowel movement) in a sibling's food while they watch (their loved one) erupt. (They do this to their loved one, for God's sake! That's nasty!) Where do they learn stuff like this? Another *hysterical* prank was to barricade the door of the smelly outhouse while camping, so the captured one had to beg and barter to be released. It cost the perpetrators all of their S'mores at the evening campfire. Once again, I was the hero!

Then there's the horrifying rumor that one of my fallen angels (or evil twin) dunked their sibling's toothbrush into the toilet out of angry spite due to a successful prank. It's not one of our finer family moments so I am going to pray to God it isn't so, and put it behind us.

Soon, kids come to figure out how valuable they can be if they band together. Their alliance can be effective when applied properly. They know moms weaken under continual pleading. When my daughter wanted a dog, she persuaded her brothers to join in on the begging and badgering even though they didn't particularly want one. So they all dropped constant reminders and suggested how great it would be to have a furry friend. They softened me like consistent licks of an ice cream cone. Eventually, Mom did cave in from the pressure and warm tongue-lashings.

His name was Hugo. I had to learn to love him. Because it was I who would come to feed him, walk him, scoop his poops...

All the years of them wishing they were an only child comes to a halt when they learn the notion that there can be strength in numbers. And when they are old enough to know how to or foolish enough to dare to plead the Fifth Amendment, they will surely try it but once. Like the time three of my bright rays of sunshine decided to take turns painting graffiti on the side of the fairly new cedar-sided garage with a can of bright fluorescent orange (*orange* mind you) spray paint they found. I almost went berserk! I had to remind myself that anything I would say or do could be used against me in a court of law so I better not leave fingerprints when I smack them! (I'm just kidding. Just testing to see if you are still paying attention. They lived to tell about it—they're fine.)

After the yelling subsided the interrogation began. It was only a matter of time until the spirit of one of the quivering children would break and the tight lips would loosen.

"Whose brilliant idea was this?" I said sweetly, trying to trick them into thinking it was a compliment.

I had to sweat out the meekest one. The eyes always give the guiltiest party away. The most innocent member would look to their leader for silent guidance. I probably wouldn't have been quite as mad if the mastermind would have at least been able to spell the graffiti correctly! I mean really, for Pete's sake! **HAV AN NIS DAE?** It was hard to stay mad at them for that. I guess they meant well.

Unfortunately, once the group finds out which one is the weak link, blabber mouth, tattle-tale, nark, snitch, big-mouth informant who will spill their guts at the first sign of pressure, he or she usually isn't to be used or trusted again in any further shenanigans. This truly becomes a blessing in disguise for both the left-out child and the parents. It always helps to have an insider who will divulge secrets about their siblings. It's amazing all the information that kids will tell you when you bribe them with a sucker. That's probably where it got its name!

The time has come when Mom has to put a sting operation into effect to bust up the gang before it is too late. They can all be bribed and bought at any age. They each have their own breaking point and it's up to you to figure out what their weakness is. Whether you tempt them with a lavender skirt and lip gloss, tricycle, pack of gum, mini bike, all the ice cream they can eat in one sitting, use of the car, pizza party or a new cell phone, they will start to see things your way.

The real trick to it is to be their friend through it all. I know that psychologists say that kids need you to be their parent not their friend. I think they're crazy. I think what kids really need is for their parents to be their parents *and* their friends! I say, keep them close to you so they tell you all of their secrets. I surely want to be one of the first to know when the beer parties are going down. Then I conveniently let the air out of their tires. I love it that my kids share all their joys, wishes and dreams with me. We swap trust, respect and sincere care and concern. Being so close allows me to guide and teach them almost without them realizing it. As they seek my advice as a valued opinion I nonchalantly encourage them into activities they show talent at beside beer bongs; suggest who might make good dating material; direct them to better-paying jobs, sensible clothes, college choices that aren't too far away, financial advice and condoms. I talk them out of ridiculous purchases, funky Mohawk hairdos that won't flatter them even on their best day, and try to get them to avoid piercings and tattoos altogether.

As for sexual encounters, those can easily be cooled by Mom staying close by, or better yet, between the spunky couple, 24/7. I encouraged them to play a lot of lengthy games of Monopoly to distract them from frisky moods. Which, years down the road, may surface as another issue. When any of them get sexually aroused, they may just feel like shopping!

I have always kept my own alliance with each of my kids. A common truce is healthy and lends for a much smoother ride. Besides, it's healthy for siblings to have a little bit of rivalry in the kingdom. It builds character and teaches them to problem-solve and how to fight fair. And if they are busy fighting with each other, they don't have energy left to fight with me, so I can do my job of ruling the roost. Then I'm the one they run to for help and protection. Mom can be firm, fair and friendly. Long live the queen!

If any of my kids hurt one another—they're all going to get it. And remember my final rule: "You're never too big or too old to be taken over Mom's knee and get a spanking! Trust me, I'll be cheerful and you'll be tearful!" But it's the *threat* of scribbling permanent-marker mustaches on them and washing their mouths out using the infamous toilet-dunked toothbrush—loaded with unconditional love—that really keeps them in line!

CHAPTER 19

Little Dickens

At an early age I learned the meaning of an important and commonly used word in our household: *dickens.* Our little dickens was my brother Brian! He had a sweet little grin that melted my mom's heart and I know his cuteness was his life-saver. That little dickens got away with plenty, much of which I will keep private because my mom will be reading this.

Brian could be very thoughtful. Like the time he crawled up onto the counter as a youngster and ate almost a whole prescription bottle of pills. When my scared mother came running into the kitchen, realizing in horror what he'd done, he handed her the container and said, "Look, Mommy, I saved you some."

Brian could also be competitive. He liked to do one bigger or one better. Like the time I had a loose tooth come out and he pulled out two of his own (which I don't really even think were loose) just to outdo me. Not to mention he liked throwing the tooth fairy a loop.

He loved the element of surprise. One time we were entertaining close friends at home. At the end of the gathering and amidst the commotion of saying good-bye, no one had noticed where he was. Brian thought it would be funny to hide behind our friends' back-seat and pop up to yell "Surprise" once they were almost all the way home. Let me tell you, he was successful, it *was* a surprise! And after they had to turn around and bring him back home I recall Dad turning shades of red that even Crayola hadn't come up with yet.

Brian could be careless and often got into trouble. Or consequently, trouble found him. During a game of hide-and-seek he hurriedly contorted himself to be upside down in the closet. Finding a large stick-pin, he put it between his teeth and, trying to get himself upright again, he sucked in and swallowed it by accident. I remember hearing my dad utter another common phrase that day: "How in the Sam Hell did that happen?" My dad didn't cuss as a rule and we didn't really even know who Sam was, but Brian usually was present when Sam's name came up.

Brian was brave. One time we were home alone and I was frightened by the creaks in the house. My over-active imagination concocted a prowler upstairs. Brian, playing along, left me at the bottom of the stairs with a hammer in one hand and a can of air freshener in the other. He instructed me that if the prowler got past him and came downstairs I should spray the stuff in his eyes and conk him on the head. He tiptoed up the steps. As I stood there petrified and ready to pounce, I listened to him move through the house until he fell, made it sound like a struggle and later claimed with that grin on his face that he chased the prowler out the back door. He was hailed as my hero before I realized he had been faking me out the whole time!

As his little sister I thank him for tricking me into eating doggie treats. It taught me resiliency. And all the times he jumped out of the closet and scared the bejesus out of me taught me how to be quick on my feet. I'm grateful for all the times we shared our love of nature, pretended we were lost in the woods and built forts, ate berries and believed we could survive there if we had to, or at least until we were called in for dinner.

I can't believe that at a very young age he influenced me to go into our neighbor Mrs. Staffenson's yard, pull the flowers out of her garden and then go to her front door and try to sell them back to her. What a scheme! Don't you think we probably should have shaken the dirt off of them first? Thank goodness it didn't lead me to a life of crime but I did gain some good sales skills from it.

Parenting Brian took skill and patience beyond all the advice that Dr. Spock could dish out. And yet I recall on countless occasions as a kid when my dad used to scold me and say that he hoped I'd have ten kids when I grew up—that were, just like me! I should have seemed like an angel after Brian, but the only explanation I have is that by the time they were done parenting him they were exhausted and overwhelmed. Well, it would appear it was a curse and my dad got his wish!

I mothered four eggs: one scrambled, one fried, one over easy and one sunny side up (not necessarily in that order). Three boys and one girl. What are the chances that three out of my four kids would be the next generation of dickens? Only, the new-age term for "dickens" is "A.D.D." The clinical name is "Attention Deficit Disorder." We lay persons call it **A**lways **D**aring & **D**efiant.

All three of my boys have A.D.D. That is three quarters of my children! 75%! We liked the odds when the nurse told me Brad had a 75% chance of not getting tetanus after stepping on a rusty nail. We felt extremely lucky when the doctor told us Ryan had a 75% chance he wouldn't lose a kidney due to a rare illness. And the 75% odds of Alex's facial scars healing from a horrible sledding accident (when his face collided with pavement) seemed like a positive outcome. But holy crap. What could I have done as a kid to deserve such fantastic odds? I should head to the casino.

My boys are extremely bright, creative, inventive, clever and innovative. They are good, kind and polite. Unfortunately as adolescents they were impulsive and reactive and, more often than not, lacking in self-control.

There were signs of it when they were very young. At times they would get in fights over the same toy. They would roll around on the floor and try to wrestle it away from one another. I'm not an advocate for violence; in fact I highly discourage it in most cases. But sometimes I'll admit I would get caught up in the excitement of seeing two males fighting over a vacuum. You just don't see that often enough!

I got accustomed to stammering strangers questioning, "Doesn't he make you nervous?" as one would hang by one ankle, up-side down, in precarious places. We've been bounced from Mc Donald's Fun Land when they slithered up to the top, got outside of the cage and propped themselves on the "No Climbing" sign. They will test every "Slippery When Wet" warning and dive into any pool with four inches of water or more just to prove a point.

They are the ones who have an obsession to push the bowling balls back down the chute. They refuse to heed warnings about electrical boxes and for some absurd reason, they like licking 9-volt batteries as shockingly warped entertainment. These are the boys that were drawn to touch every fire exit just to watch Mommy squirm. They invented danger by snowboarding behind a snow-mobile pulled by a tow-rope and dared to hang onto a firework's fuse as long as they could. They truly could make a sane woman go crazy. It might be too late in fact!

Their attention spans were short and they had selective hearing. They never seemed to hear requests or demands about homework or chores and yet they always remembered where to find the hidden cookies in the house. They apparently couldn't comprehend safety rules but miraculously were able to figure out how to power any motor, gear, switch, gadget or lever to make motion.

Each of them took approximately 107 reminders per day to stay on task. This included scolding to not ingest disgusting things, and being coaxed down from death-defying heights or out of compromising places. I had to prod them to apologize for erratic behaviors and impulsive outbursts. Evidently it is much harder to teach children to censor their own mouths than it is to impress upon them the importance of covering their germy sneezes. I read them their Miranda rights often.

Many days quite ordinary in nature I received phone calls from fellow parents wanting to share the tales of my boys' behavior. Once it was a girl's jacket that was launched onto the roof of the school. One call was about my undernourished child using another kid's lunch card to get free desserts. Another time one son persuaded a neighbor girl to ride their bikes for miles just to get some candy at the store then realized in the check-out lane they forgot to bring money. Another day Junior and friends went joy-riding down the road on a borrowed (oops! forget to ask for the owner's permission) golf cart. Or the time when my youngster took a plastic comb to school that resembled a switchblade and got into huge trouble. That was another "What were you thinking?" moment. Precisely why mothers get gray hair!

Unfortunately, I have met several parents in our community by dragging my child to their front door to plead for clemency. Embarrassed and apologetic, I assure these parents that my boys were not bad kids or holy terrors, nor were they misguided, but acted with the impulse of self-indulged comedic adolescents who value a laugh higher than common sense. These parents usually found no humor in the situation and rarely were they laughing.

Imagine a kid taking a shopping cart loaded with enough food to feed a family of six for two and a half weeks, pushing it haphazardly down the sloped center aisle of a parking lot and let go. I'm sure watching me dart the twenty-yard dash in 3.7 seconds, retrieving the cart just moments before it crashed into a parked car, was probably hysterical. It's amazing I didn't take up drinking!

How would you like to get a startling call at work about your teenage boy who was playing dodge-the-BB in the woods with a buddy? Evidently he zigged when he should have zagged because a BB ricocheted off a tree and shot him! The damn ammunition was embedded in his lower lip for gosh sakes. Thanks to me for investing $4,200 to install those bulletproof braces that effectively stopped the BB from going down his throat. It's not every day one needs to leave work early because her son got shot. Yes! They could have taken an eye out! "How many times have I told you…?" I'm going to have to switch to a darker shade to cover all this gray hair!

Now, this may sound sexist, but I am confident in saying that boys will be boys. Nicole has done some pretty quirky things over the years and her halo has slid and nearly fell off a couple of times. But I can honestly say that she never once showed an interest in what was under a manhole cover, sewer grate or an animal's tail. She never shoved things into our exhaust pipe just to see if they would launch upon acceleration. She loves the heights of a roller coaster and the daring speed of a jet ski but never once did she attempt to climb the bags of fertilizer piled high on pallets at the garden center or shimmy up a display ladder. She never tried to jam the checkout conveyer belt with coins or switch gears on the car while we were driving.

If I told her not to do something because it might hurt or she'd get into trouble, that was convincing enough. She never lifted the lid on the blender in motion or overflowed the toilet on purpose. Nor do I recollect her defying my advice and then while brushing herself off adamantly argue that "That didn't hurt" or "I knew that would happen!"

Whether it is genetics producing the next generation of dickens or an A.D.D. coincidence, it is safe to say I was gifted with all of the testosterone I could possibly handle. Or maternally speaking, a better term might be that I was blessed with my three little deviled eggs!

CHAPTER 20
Beneath The Seat

Loading the big yellow bus floods back memories from my childhood. The steps are still too high and the narrow aisle is another reminder to diet, but the rows of seats, even from my adult perspective, go on forever. Once we established our voluntary seating, most kids were vying for my attention to have me sit by them, while my own child, Alex, sat in a seat all alone, two rows back, and barely acknowledged I was there. We began our field trip by pondering why it's called a "field trip" anyway. If we were going to a farm or a soccer game it might be appropriate but the museum isn't in a field!

The teacher counts all sixty-one heads of the second grade class, most of which you can hardly see the tops of over the big green vinyl backrests. She reminds the children that our journey is long and there are no rest rooms along the way. She gives me my chaperone assignment: I'm responsible for keeping track of five little seven-year-old kids: Jayden, Gavin, Korren, my son Alex and Olivia. *I'm a veteran, I should be able to handle this,* I thought.

After three verses of "The Wheels on the Bus Go Round and Round", Alex discovers what fun I can be and wants to now worm his way in next to me, causing a slight re-arrangement. Jayden is discontented with his new partner and begins to wince.

"He's touching me," he whines in an indescribable tone.

"It's okay, there's room for everybody. We'll be there soon," I lie as we round the corner out of the school parking lot with about forty-eight minutes to go. This is the same child that I witnessed earlier who reached down underneath the bottom of his seat, pried off a piece of dried-out bubble gum (and who knows how long it had been stuck there, probably by some rebel) then proceeded to pop it into his mouth trying to revive some flavor out of it. And he's worried that his elbow may catch some disease by brushing another kid's jacket?

By verse seventeen we're babbling. I untangle Korren's bracelet clasp from the fur on her coat.

"Take one down and pass it around," I blurt out, then catch a stern look from a teacher and realize I'm on the wrong tour bus for that song.

Olivia and Korren play a robust round of a pat-a-cake type of game, slapping and clapping their hands to sing-song lyrics. They giggle with delight as they prattle through their modern-day rap song. Alex is crouched between the seats, reaching underneath to grab at Gavin's feet. Gavin gets mad which only makes Alex all the more pleased with himself. Jayden is negotiating a trade of his ABC gum to another recipient for a piece of peppermint which that other boy found, slightly lint-covered, stuck inside his pocket. Before I could foil the transaction, the trade took place behind the seat and I could see it was a done deal as the empty wrapper floated to the bus floor.

The combined volume from all of the silliness of singing, laughing and talking made my own voice inaudible at times. My bladder bounced as the tail end of the bus jolted us over every bump in the road like a bronco ride. It was then that I realize that my morning coffee had caught up with me and I really had to go to the little girls' room. I was afraid that if I laughed too hard while being catapulted out of my seat the landing might cause the urine-induced disaster my doctor warned me about. I silently began my Kegel exercises as a preventative measure.

Finally we arrived at the museum. The devoted singers up front wound down with "N-G-O and Bingo is his name-o." The teacher sent us on our way with instructions and gave our groups freedom to roam independently. I like the idea until we are standing in front of the ladies' room and I'm the only adult around. Taking my position very seriously, not wanting to lose anyone's child I make them all hold hands. Korren hung onto the stall handle and the rest hung onto ends of their scarves to create a long line with the boys straggling out the bathroom door. Going as fast as I could, I heard Jayden announce to passers-by that his dad said he is too old to go into the girls' bathroom and shouldn't go in there. Everyone takes their turn in the washroom and meets outside in the hall. Except for Jayden who was testing me to see if I was too old to go into the men's room! I most definitely am, but it was the only way to get him out. There was only one elderly curator in there who I think was from the original King Tut tomb. He was busy circling his foot trying to get some paper unstuck from his shoe so I doubt he even noticed me in there.

"What shall we see first?" I asked excitedly.

Olivia and Gavin wanted to see the live butterfly exhibit and pulled my arm in that direction. Alex was already heading down the hall toward the pyramid. Korren was drawn to the Native American drums rumbling in the distance and was telling me about a beautiful costume she saw around the corner. Jayden took a stance and claimed no matter what he was not going into the jungle area if there were snakes in there.

It cost me three pieces of licorice, the promise of ice cream treats, and a granola bar for Gavin who was lactose-intolerant to get them all to agree to stick together. We would start in the butterfly wing. I had to wipe away Jayden's huge tears with my sleeve and convince the poor terrified kid that Alex was kidding;

there really weren't snakes in the butterfly exhibit. Alex ran ahead and was inside already being scolded by a museum employee for grabbing at the butterflies.

"They will land on you if you are patient," she insisted.

Korren stood perfectly still. Olivia kept trying to reach out when one fluttered nearby. Gavin got so excited each time a big, beautiful moth came near, wanting to land on his blond curls, that his glee scared them away. Korren became frustrated that none of them would land on her, when she was trying so hard. Earlier I had set my backpack down on a tree-trunk bench while I tried to place myself in an active viewing spot. Another group from a different school joined us and one child quickly crawled up and squatted on top of my backpack, which had our lunches tucked carefully inside.

One of the juice boxes burst open and was dripping through the canvas. As I tried to rearrange the lunch items away from the torn, soggy bags and mop up the spill I realized that boredom had afflicted Gavin and Korren. I spotted them through the glass outside of the exhibit area. I worked my way through the crowd to catch up with them. Olivia immediately sensed we were going and instinctively clung to my side as I went out the door to retrieve the other two. The alarm sounded due to the valuable insect I was inadvertently smuggling out, perched on the strap of my knapsack. It probably smelled the sweet nectar seeping through our belongings.

As I yelled over my shoulder trying to get the meandering children's attention and regain leadership, the guard led me back inside the exhibit so that I could return the endangered species, with Olivia clutching my left thigh the whole time. I apologized to her after I stepped on her foot once or twice, trying to move quickly as I looked for Alex and called to Jayden to come with us. He was mesmerized and didn't want to leave. I couldn't see Alex anywhere.

I jerked my head back out in the hall to see if he had joined the others. Then I spotted him hiding under some huge leaves pretending to be a snake as Jayden approached him. I tried to intervene but was a second too late as Jayden came face-to-face with Alex who was sticking out his tongue and hissing. Jayden screamed and startled all of the butterflies, which took flight in a frenzy. Olivia thought it was silly but I just lowered my head in shame at the glaring looks of disgust from the other chaperones. I grabbed both boys by the collar and, with Olivia in tow, escorted them to the door where I twirled them each around three times to dislodge any winged refugees. We then poured into the hall to seek out my two delinquent followers. Much to my relief, we were once again reunited just in time as their teacher came around the corner.

"Are you all having a good time?" she inquired.

"We're having a ball," I said as calmly as I could muster. *About as much fun as a flu shot,* I thought to myself.

We were heading to the giant-screen theater for a show with the rest of the class. It had to be much easier to keep five seven-year-olds confined to their seats. *I'll lie across their laps if I have to.* The movie begins and Korren whispers, "Alex's mom, I don't feel good." She looked green from motion sickness. We scurry up the steep staircase to find a bathroom. We make it to the throne in time, but she says she feels fine by then. She has a sip of water and we return to the theater. Back inside I can look down to our aisle and see Alex in the shadows. He once again was defying the confines of his seat by climbing out and sitting on the steps. It's apparent now, we really need to review his medicine dose.

Gavin was playing with Olivia's pigtails. She would then whip her head around which would slap the tail across his face. They laughed. I hurried to get back to my post to keep some order when

Korren saw the image on the massive screen move. She moaned as she turned around and headed out, covering her mouth with her hand. That time sounded for real.

After getting some air she appeared fine once again. By then the movie had ended. Korren and I headed back down to our seats to gather our things and join the rest of our gang. We fought against the traffic of the rest of the people who were rushing up the steps to get to the lunchroom to eat. We passed Jayden who was anxious to get to lunch but I turned him around to follow us. Alex tried to continue to sit in the aisle to make pedestrians trip and step over him as a weird sort of game.

After another set of bribes that would cost me dearly and an additional lecture about good behavior, I led my troops on to lunch. Every stitch of bread in our knapsack was soggy and tainted with orange drink. Olivia wasn't giggling any more. Korren whined that she was thirsty. It was her drink that exploded so she somehow got blamed for it by Jayden. Gavin shared his drink. Alex thought it was amusing that his ham sandwich was orange until he got a glimpse of his bloated stick pretzels that resembled worms. They all got grossed out then! I suggested we move on and pick up a snack later.

As we cleaned up our table, I noticed that Jayden was getting spots on his face, neck and arms that were the same shade as the brilliantly red hair on his head.

"I think I'm not supposed to have orange juice," he blurted out in his sweet little voice.

"Oh….no," was the most brilliant response I could come up with that didn't include an expletive.

Jayden could see that I felt really sad about it so he tried to comfort me by saying, "It's okay, this happened lots of times already. My dad keeps forgetting too."

Gavin crinkled up his nose and laughed to himself as we viewed the polka dots on Jayden's arm. Alex, in awe, stood still and quiet for the longest time his mouth was hanging open in puzzlement. Olivia backed up a step and asked if she would catch them. Korren added to the anxiety by claiming that she couldn't get sick because she had a dance recital to perform in and her dad said they paid an arm and a leg for her costume and if she missed the recital she would have to wear it every day until she grew out of it.

After a long explanation from their teacher about hives and a reassurance that no one will catch anything from anyone, I guided us out toward some bizarre tribal wear in the hallway that hopefully would distract them.

"He'll be just fine," I say convincingly.

We had a little time before we had to meet up with the bus so I'd made the decision to go to the American Indian exhibit. I knew we would all like that. In the buffalo display there was a snake with a tail that rattled when Alex pressed a button. The girls gave a satisfying scream but Jayden put up a tough front. His face turned red which made the hives momentarily blend in, but he never lost his cool as he stayed safely tucked behind me.

Gavin scurried around the rotating circular display of life-sized, costumed dancers, mimicking their moves. Korren pointed to a mannequin which she claimed looked so much like her grandfather that it was almost creepy. Olivia was pretending to play the drums on a nearby railing. I hurried around the display like a hamster on a wheel, trying to catch up with Gavin. He unexpectedly had turned a corner and came upon an exhibit featuring bare-breasted women. He looked embarrassed as he announced it shyly to the others. The pandemonium began.

With a laugh I suggested that this year, when it came to

pick a deserving family to donate holiday gifts to, the school should choose those poor ladies in the exhibit. Trying to distract their attention to something else was impossible. Jayden's big round eyes had a surprised look, like he'd struck gold. Giggling, the kids chattered on about sewing and donating clothes. Alex offered to contribute Nicole's bras and Korren wanted to leave her jacket to cover up at least one of them. Olivia's giggles trailed off as (trying to regain some composure) I drove my troop out of the area.

We scurried to catch our large yellow mode of transportation. I was checking and rechecking that I had all of my disciples and their belongings. Once we were settled in, it was a relatively quiet ride home except for the brief commotion in the rear. One student kept poking the blunt arrows (purchased in the museum gift shop) into another child's leg. A teacher confiscated the arrows which was a wise but unpopular decision. Many of the kids cast the looks of demons at her back as she returned to her seat and grumbled that if they didn't behave, there was a very good chance her son would get them as a birthday present. My group was tired and Jayden's mild case of hives had almost disappeared by the time we got back to school and his waiting mother.

A few singers lingered with E-I-E-I-O. Preparing to gather all our belongings, I inventoried the multiple pairs of mittens, one set of earmuffs, one blue knit hat, and a pink scarf that was wet on one end from being stepped on in the aisle. Alex's spiked hair was the only part of him that still looked perky. Korren stroked the fur on her coat as if it were a real pet. Gavin rested his forehead on the steamed window, looking for his mother. I counted five heads one final time, gave each member of my crew a hug and thanked them for inviting me to come.

Olivia repeatedly whipped her limp pigtails in anyone's face she could get close enough to and laughed out loud. Her hair caught a clump of saliva-covered gum in one boy's mouth and it was yanked out clinging to the end of her hair. The boy, hoping for some empathy from a chaperone, whined, "She took my gum."

Realizing what had just happened, Olivia did not want to get into trouble. She instantly snatched the gum off the ends of her hair. She quickly looked around and without hesitation took the wad of gum in her petite fingertips and slipped it back under the seat from which it came.

Speechless and frankly a little stunned, I clutched my damp, sticky backpack and went home to take a bath with my box of wine propped on the side of the tub. I have come to believe that teachers are saints for their ability to endure that kind of chaos every day. Their commitment is remarkable. I am amazed you don't see more of them at AA meetings.

I revel in the memory of the last school outing I ever took. But even more importantly, at least I now know the profound explanation of the gum beneath the seat.

CHAPTER 21

Superstar

I never imagined that a hip, trendy and youthful parent such as myself could ever become stricken by a generational gap. I mean really— how could twenty years make that much difference? I try extremely hard to walk the walk, and talk the talk, but aside from the normal parent—teen discrepancies, the relationships I have with each of my four kids are really quite close. But I think it would be safe to say that my teenagers admire me from afar. The key word here is "afar."

Parents have varying degrees of motivation in guiding their children's success. The real test for parents is when one of our offspring becomes involved in a sport or competition of any kind. For some adults it's enough that their kids go out for football or try pole-vaulting as a way to gain knowledge in a sport. Others encourage their kids to get involved in wrestling or the synchronized swim team to gain social skills. (We know it certainly must build character and confidence to be able to walk around in public in unflattering suits and caps like that.) There are a fair number of parents who are driven to get their children into ice-skating or gymnastics because they believe there is Olympic blood in their kid's veins; gaining notoriety on a Wheaties box would be the ultimate outcome. A portion is motivated by the greedy thoughts of financial reward if their kid should succeed as a professional boxer or baseball player. Others find satisfaction in filling their trophy cases and walls with equestrian plaques and ribbons of achievement. I have witnessed many parents just trying to fill the void, wanting their kids to excel at sports in general because they themselves failed at it miserably. Let's face it; nobody wants their child to be the last one picked when choosing sides.

But for me, I can honestly say it is pretty unselfish. I just like good, clean fun. I'm willing to admit what I lack in athleticism I make up with enthusiasm. My commitment to team spirit and good sportsmanship notwithstanding, it takes all the strength and self-control I've got to not get too emotionally involved and so competitively charged that I personally want to knock (gently of course) each opponent out of my child's way, just so I can see him or her succeed. In fact I would carry (or drag if I had to) my athlete's weary, dehydrated body across any finish line just so he could say, "I did it!" No matter how foolish I looked.

Having said that, the season was soccer and the sidelines was where I promised to stay. Oh, and one additional little promise I made to my teenager…to be quiet and not embarrass him. I could do that. I could respect his wishes and not cause a scene or call undue attention to myself. I just get caught up in the excitement once in awhile, that's all. But my intentions were very good.

As I settled into the small crowd of spectators along the field, with my toes just to the white painted line, I secured the hood on my feather-filled jacket and placed it precisely out of my peripheral vision but high enough on my head to cover my ears. The brisk fall air caused my hands to plant themselves inside the corners of my pockets. My shoulders automatically rounded up to create a wind block for my already cold face and protruding red nose. During the pre-game chit chat with other parents, the warm exhaled air from our mouths was immediately snatched away by the northerly current. Sniffling noses was a common background sound and could almost be used as a countdown to the start of the game.

I saw the high-school coach peer over his shoulder to find me in attendance. Our eye contact gave me an uneasy feeling about the phone call I made to him earlier that week. It was our little secret. He hadn't been fairly using all of the players that were on the bench and I reminded him that my son got up at 5 a.m. and made it to every practice date, worked hard and was eagerly determined to play. It's only a high-school level of game and everyone should have a fair chance, I'd told the coach. We weren't going for professional status or the Heisman trophy for goodness sake. It probably didn't hurt that I reminded him that ultimately I (as a taxpayer) pay his salary…Lo and behold: my son was on the field!

I looked across the field and saw my pride and joy head-to-head with his opponent. In a ruckus of contrasting team colors vying for position and control I shockingly witnessed what seemed to be a red-blooded, all-American kid, blatantly and physically cause a penalty against my blood relative. I was, at that point, emotionally involved!

I wanted to have a talk with that kid. My squinting eyes scanned across the soccer field to see if I could pick his parents out of the lineup. I'd like to suggest they consider enrolling him in anger management therapy for having such aggressively competitive behavior. I started down the sidelines in the slalom race of my life; quickly I weaved in and out of the other spectators.

"Excuse me, excuse me!" Each time I pleaded, my pitch and volume rose.

I spotted my precious first-born face down and motionless in the dirt.

"Are you all right?" I hollered. (Who needs a megaphone?) The game had stopped in its tracks, and a few heads turned toward me. I held my breath for many long moments. Finally his still body began to move. No doubt hearing my voice was like a whiff of smelling salts. I sighed with relief as my star player regained an upward position and a will to live. He had a look of retaliation I'd never seen before. He wasn't going to get mad; he was going to get even by scoring a goal!

The clock was still ticking and the play resumed. My exceptional child magically maneuvered around that pathetic little brute who had just abused him and plowed past. Caught up in the excitement I began to scream, "All *right!* Squash that little…—" Thank goodness I caught myself before I finished my sentence. Trying to compose myself, instead of screaming I swiftly smacked my gloved hands together making a muted clap of enthusiasm.

Accidentally, my son's name slipped out again and, well, quite a few more times while I ran back up the field following the play. My toes carefully teetered on the outside of the painted guidelines, just as I promised. I awkwardly tripped over a couple of parents along the way (I wondered who could sit at a time like that). I looked back to check that they were okay. They waved and nodded as they recovered. There was an unspoken understanding between us. In the meantime my superstar had taken control of the game and was no longer an anonymous player, thanks to me.

The game continued as the autumn air turned my son's cold bare thighs pink. He had turf crammed behind the laces in his shoes and grass stain smudges on his uniform; his knee-socks were slipping down over his shin guards.

He seemed to be tired but focused. His team had fought to control and moved the ball as their legs of fury kicked feverishly. Finally the game ended with an exuberant victory. The tired but excited warriors had achieved a deserving win and the final score was a beautifully scripted team effort.

I felt it was necessary to support the apple of my eye with additional boisterous and encouraging words. While chanting to our victorious team, the fans escorted them across the tundra toward the locker room entrance. I congratulated the coach, beaming in an I-told-you-so way. Slowly the group dwindled as we scattered to the warmth in our vehicles. I waited in the lot for my

#1 player who emerged from the building. My emotions were contained once again.

Ryan climbed into the car and slouched down in the seat with the hood of his heavyweight sweatshirt pulled over his head and the long sleeves concealing his hands. All I could see were his eyes rolling at me as I patted him on the back and exclaimed, "Great game today!"

"You're so embarrassing! Do you have to be yelling and cheering all the time? Can't I get a ride to the next game with someone else's parents?" he muttered with a partial chuckle. He knew in his heart that I meant well but I just couldn't control my childlike excitement.

"No, you're stuck with me. And besides, I stayed on the sidelines the whole time just like you asked and I wasn't *that* loud!" It was hard to plead my case with a voice that was hoarse from yelling.

"Yeah, at least you didn't come running out onto the field like last time, pulling that stupid first-aid kit out of your purse," he replied sarcastically.

I ignored the comment and said, "You showed 'em today, you were awesome!"

He couldn't contain the smile of satisfaction that slowly crept across his face. I knew he felt pretty good. I'm proud of my mature player because it was great sportsmanship that made him better than most. As for the rest of us we must remember it's just a game. Games should be fun and fair. All kids of any age should get a chance to play.

Ryan grew out of the sport and his interests took him to other places. But for me, my love of the athletic challenge and camaraderie continues. You can still find me on the sidelines of Alex's soccer games. But now I'm the coach, so I have a license to yell as much as I want as I root for everybody's kids. Trust me, all of our "Superstars" will get a chance to play… but the sidelines are mine!

"Excuse me, excuse me! Please get out of my way!"

CHAPTER 22
Public Displays of Nudity (PDN)

It's winter! I insist on trying not to hate the cold frozen waste-land that I live in. I do love the beauty of a new-fallen snow covering the horizon, when every twig or branch balances a collection of beautiful sparkling freeze-dried crystals. Instead of fighting the chapped lips, dry skin and nasal drip that won't ease up until the end of March, I aim to be optimistic and go with it. I don my sexy bib snow pants, knit ski mask that snarls my long locks, and boots that thud when I walk… and head out to play with Alex. After making therapeutic snow angels we licked some polluted snow off our gloves. We waited as long as we could for the icicles hanging from the garage gutter to drip in our open mouths. There is a promise of hot chocolate and a warmly lit fire to thaw our fingers and toes when we are through. Ah! To be a kid again!

In the Midwest we do everything in a big way. One year by December 4th I had already snow-blown the driveway seven times. The battery in my truck had needed its annual jump-start while stranded on the shoulder of a country road. Brad drove over with his jumper cables and saved the day. He owed me though, as I with mighty chains and my four-wheel-drive SUV had retrieved his car from a ditch not once but twice that season already.

Alex took his first snowboarding lesson on Wednesday of that week while Brad a veteran, was laid up on Friday after cracking two ribs performing a spectacular stunt (he almost landed) trying to perfect the same sport. I wish they built hospitals with a glide-in clinic at the base of ski hills and half-pipe runs to ease transporta-tion and hassle. Our doctor already has my number on his speed dial and I have faxed my parental authorization giving permission for treatment. Now all I need is for the hospital to sell gift certificates so I could provide my kids with pre-paid coverage for mishaps. Then the hospital could mend them and send them home in a taxi.

Nicole and my two grandsons stopped by to borrow a shovel. She needed to shovel out her other car that was stuck, blocking a whole apartment building parking lot, before it would be towed away. Their visit was just long enough that we had to scramble to re-dress the kids from head to foot. Two pairs of duplicate gloves with matching scarves, four boots, two hats, snow pants and jackets for each. Finally they were bundled and ready to go. Then one of them got a chill when the door opened and announced his immediate need to relieve himself (which he vowed he didn't have to do 182 seconds earlier when I asked him). I busily peeled away the layers of outerwear while he pranced, clutching his parts.

I couldn't get the clasp on one boot open, so his snow gear dangled around the ankle of one leg, bunched over the boot. He dragged it along the floor to the bathroom. He took care of business then shuffled back to me. As I re-assembled his outfit I could see some pee had trickled down his leg into his boot. If I covered it quickly I knew the liquid would stay warm like a tropical current for some time, at least until they got home. There were *only* four and a half more months of this winter wonderland to go. I was so ready for a vacation!

Water park, you say? Wisconsin does simulated summer like no other. Giant slides, lazy rivers, water cannons, tubing, hot tubs (we like to emphasize the "hot"), heated pools, spewing geysers, tide pools with make-believe surf. All that fun inside a multi-level, humidity-engulfed winter playground. Seeing the snow outside through the massive glass windows makes it all the more awesome. It is a true getaway weekend!

Upon our arrival the hotel staff slapped plastic bar-code bracelets tightly around our wrists, with a "Don't you dare take it off" warning. Now instead of "Put it on my bill" it's "Charge it to my bracelet." The concept is very handy and practical. My kids especially liked it that I no longer had to dig change out from a soggy plastic baggie that was usually pinned to the inside of my swimsuit like I was nine years old. It's a little hard to look cool though. I watched one stud trying to buy drinks for women at the bar. You can hardly take a man seriously when he's got a brightly colored vinyl ID bracelet on. It looks like something that should be used as public humiliation devices for criminals!

Yikes! The reality that I'd have to publicly expose my scantily clad, almost naked body hit. I'm grateful that our modern-day two-piece swimsuits for the mature woman consist of more than strings and small triangles of fabric, but they are revealing just the same. I hadn't held my stomach muscles in since a sweatshirt glided over my midsection in late September. Sucking it in for two whole days will surely give me gas.

There is always the need for a quick assessment around the facility to see that I am not the chubbiest or biggest-boned person in attendance. It proves to be an ego booster. I thankfully was not the biggest one there. She was wearing at least a decade old high-school issued swimsuit that looked many sizes too small and she appeared to lack exercise in her daily life. Yet she strutted with the confidence of a runway model. Aside from a few young, shapely and pubescent figures I have to admit that most of us looked like we were trying to stuff way too much filler into our bloated spandex suits.

Oh well, what the hell! More power to us all for having the guts to publicly expose so much of our self-conscious selves just for fun! Besides, I remind myself, I don't look too bad for someone who's given birth to four babies. I do the math: a 47-pound weight gain for an 8-pound, 10-ounce baby means my uterus must weigh about 36 pounds, right? That must be why I can't lose the weight.

The strong fumes of chlorine are a reminder that the place could be a cesspool of germs. I kept trying to divert my attention away from the thought of all who had used that water before us and had they washed their hands before jumping in? I tried to ignore the toddlers in sagging diapers, frisky couples in the hot tub and saliva-covered chins of children gasping for air. I threw all caution to the wind and jumped in; reassuring myself that chlorine kills everything but a good time!

We started in the tame, lazy river to get used to the water. There is no graceful way for a middle-aged woman to climb onto an inner tube. Immersing one's butt into the hole of a plastic donut seems like a simple challenge that should take little energy, if any. I started out with a wacky balancing act on all fours, spinning wildly on my bronco. My swimsuit's purpose of concealing my body failed. I was either oozing up over the top or slipping out the bottom at that point. Poise was relinquished when I realized my widest, er, asset was sticking up like a beached whale. I quickly tried to flip over hoping gravity would bring me straight down into the hole. After many attempts and all dignity lost, I too surfaced, gurgling for air with spit on my chin. If I had drowned at that point I'm sure my mother would have written an obituary stating that the cause of death was probably a cramp because I must not have waited the full hour after lunch before returning to the water.

Whistles started to blow as the water current carried me along the channel next to my flotation device.

"Ma'am, ma'am, you must be on an inner tube. Those are the rules," the young, bone-dry hunk of a lifeguard calls over to me.

Trying to preserve any cuteness I had left, I wiped the mascara off my cheekbones and batted my eyelashes free of excess droplets. I softened the shark fin swirl of hair on top my head and I brushed some wet bangs back onto my forehead. My family had drifted away and I had no one to laugh with which added to my embarrassment. By this point two alarmed lifeguards were walking the edge of the river, scowling at me. They surely weren't laughing at the thought of them having to jump in after me, all for minimum wage!

It was time to take charge. I threw my leg up onto the side of the shoulder-high concrete bank and hooked the heel of my foot on top of the abrasive wall, but the current kept on dragging me. With water up my nose, I clutched my life raft with one arm while the jagged cement scraped the skin off my foot. I think I invented a new Pilates position. My tube spun around, wedging me in, next to a relaxed kindergartener comfortably sprawled across her mode of transportation. Seizing the opportunity of excess current in a stalled pattern, I shoved my foot down to the bottom and thrust my body upward in a pole vaulter's arch to clear the brim and slid into the center of my tube. Relieved to have finally conquered the battle of the bulge, I looked to the youngster for approval. She, however, was caught in the tidal wave caused by my abrupt plunge and was hanging on for dear life while being whisked ahead. Still spinning in circles, I ignored the looks of the other people who passed by.

I was feeling a little smug. I sure showed those lifeguards that I could rise to the occasion! Then I thought, "Did that young punk just *ma'am* me?"

Coming around the last turn, I spot my kids who had long finished their lazy float and were on dry land, quite anxious to try something a little more daring. I felt that I deserved to continue experiencing the relaxation of the ride so I told them I'd catch up with them on the body surf rides in a bit. As I embarked on my second lap of the lazy river, I relaxed all my tired muscles and took in the sights for a short while. I reveled in the carefree activity of Public Displays of Nudity (PDN). I found that dangling my half-covered derriere', which was hidden from view but in a public place nonetheless was quite relaxing after all.

The winding waterway took us under a balcony filled with spectators, looking down at us. I didn't let even their gawking spoil the moment. Then I glanced out the plate-glass window and caught a reflection of my pasty-white skin that hadn't seen the light of day in months, which made my purple toenail polish stand out all the more. I was horrified at the thought of what I might look like from above. My sumo-wrestler thighs and upper arms were smooshed against the sides of my ride, doubling their size, if you know what I mean. And my cleavage gushing out my top was so impressive that I could feel the concession stand attendant's eyes burning down at me as he waited for one false move or a tsunami.

Filled with anxiety, I knew if I could raise myself up on my elbows and away from my body, the muscles in my arms would tighten, causing them to look much leaner. Next, I flattened out my tummy by slightly arching my back. Now sort of perching on top of the tube, I flexed my thighs by extending my legs out in front of me and pointing my toes. I also sucked in baby fat and held my breath as much of the way as possible. The stress of my dismount was approaching. I was almost weary from working so hard at trying to be lazy!

It was the end of the line. With a nod to the next recipient, waiting for my plastic donut, I assumed a now-or-never attitude, then did a spiral half-twist and flopped out, trying to surface with plenty of splashing to disguise the lack of gracefulness. I threw in a fancy little synchronized swimmer's kick with pointed toe to make it all appear deliberate. Completely immersed in water I finally felt thin.

Inconspicuously, I tucked and folded as much of me as I could back into the suit that had done little to flatter me. Sucking in and clinching muscles that were attempting to hold on to my abdominal wall and conceal my oversized uterus, I tried to swiftly glide across the simulated beach. I swirled inside of my giant beach towel and finally let out a well-deserved exhale.

The water slides would be my next thrill. Lord knows I have enough equipment for that sport. You must abandon all insecurities while you allow a gush of water to flush you down an eight-story tubular slide that resembles the pipe works of a toilet. Mimicking my son's moves, I laid on my back stick-straight, crossed my ankles, one arm over my chest, plugged my nose and stumbled through an abridged "Hail Mary" prior to the plunge. Alex and I, ready on side-by-side slides, smiled at each other in anticipation. All but the enema landing when our butts skidded to a stop at the bottom of the pool was invigorating. The force was so great I swear I saw water shoot out Junior's ears. We were both left with thong bottoms and I, additionally, had a neck-scarf top—and those were not water wings floating on the surface. More accidental PDN! The lifeguard was in awe. No doubt disappointed he hadn't witnessed a perkier pair, he looked away grinning. At least he'd viewed more than his wage promised. Once again, tucking my birthday suit and pride back inside my swimwear, I then climbed up the ladder.

Later, we all joined up to play in the kiddie area. Alex and my grandsons were having a ball sliding down the water slides that stopped them abruptly at the bottom mat, causing a surge of water to back-wash their little faces. We all laughed with delight, especially when one landing caused one grandson's little swimmer diaper to split up the side seam. Soon it fell to his ankles with thank heavens, nothing but wetness inside. The chlorine valve discharged a quick dose. He continued prancing, nude and free of all inhibitions.

Part of me wished I had the guts to jump out of my own suit which restricted my movement and airways. But then, thank goodness, my sensible guardian angel threw in thoughts of the family humiliation that would result, startling me out of my daydream. The authorities would drag me out in handcuffs and the media would have a field day. The headline would read: **Woman Caught Publicly Displaying Too Much Nudity! Needs to put at least two pieces back on.** But having my mug-shot taken in a swimsuit and posted in post offices would be the most humiliating of all. I am awfully hard on myself, aren't I?

My tall, slender daughter strolled over to scoop up her son with his cute little, bare tush. She could be on the advertisement flyer for the water park. She is shapely, busty and beautiful in a bikini. She is the reason many of the lifeguards were there, hoping she would lose her suit or need their lifesaving air. Little do they know her mom assisted her with double knots in her bikini strings. They won't be feasting on her PDN if I have anything to say about it. Nicole has long legs that go on forever and her stomach is still almost flat even after giving birth twice. She is the envy of all women in the place, including me. It certainly isn't genetics. I've given my daughter many things but luckily she didn't get her figure from me and apparently she wasn't gifted with the heredity of big bones or a huge uterus either!

CHAPTER 23

True Love: I'm Finally in My Happy Place

I was always a gushing girl with Cinderella Syndrome. It wasn't that my view of love was distorted; my parents set the perfect example as the epitome of a loving married couple. In an era when waiting to be chosen and taken home like a puppy from the pound was the norm, to me relationship roles were the mystery. As an impressionable young female I was somewhat passive and naïve which often led me straight into disaster. I wasn't yet an independent woman, who would make choices and decisions that would steer my own future.

I was slightly ill-equipped as a young woman, without ample information about mating. It's a science as to how to detect the right fish in the sea. The second pea to my pod. And there was something about a butcher, a baker and a candlestick maker that had me confused. Then there was that truly puzzling rumor about couples who stay together long enough begin to look alike. Holy crap, that's just frightening!

Cinderella was my only relatable rags-to-riches character. I believe in magic and the wondrous way the spirit can overcome adversity. I nurture an overwhelming optimism that love can conquer all. I'm a hopeful romantic to the core who yearns for TLC and happy endings. My imaginary hope chest consisted of glass slippers, pumpkins and a couple of caged mice destined to become stallions. I was tempted by poisonous apples, dangled my long hair out the window often and kissed every frog I found in the bog, hoping for the fairy tale to turn into reality.

I dared my knight to sweep me off my feet. I was ready, willing and able to be smitten. I was blinded by gobs of infatuation. I eagerly swooned with passion. My soul mate would breathe life into my veins and drench me with affection. My prince would fulfill my sense of security by protecting me from all harm. We would be complete, happily ever after!

Startled as my nodding forehead tapped the screen on my computer monitor—I abruptly woke up! I lift my dozing head. The heavy eyelids over my tired bloodshot eyes, attempt to blink and provide refreshed vision. Certain that my Romeo is out there somewhere, I plod on to study the next singles applicant on Match.com. It isn't exactly how I had it romantically planned out in my mind.

I used to joke about mail-order brides. I certainly never thought it would become a method by which I would test my fate and match personal similarities like a game-show contestant. However, it's the twenty-first century and everyone is doing it, my friend Cheryl reassures me.

First I had to compile a profile that would help me stand out above my competition. I spent hours both spilling out the sordid details of my life and deciding which quirky tales should become surprises for later. Probably the fact that I lied on my profile about liking erotica (I knew it would get their attention) and I suppose eventually I will have to explain about the seven little old men I keep in the guesthouse.

I searched through boxes of photos to find a flattering portrait of myself. After it was cropped and airbrushed, I looked gorgeous! He'll just have to take my mom's word for it that my weight is proportionate to my height. And just why is that so damned important to guys anyway? Some of them should invest in a full-length mirror for themselves!

Lastly, to complete my personal data I had to boast about my most favorable personality traits and add enticing details. Of course I had to leave out any mention of annoying dislikes such as my aversion to feet (mine or anyone else's). There will be absolutely *no touching* and, heaven forbid, *no sucking of feet!* Or I'll have my two nasty stepsisters lock him in the tower as punishment.

Finally, I created a perky title for myself. And then, it was time to wait for a response and reel in Mr. Charming.

It was easy getting caught up in the excitement of receiving email each day. I was anxious to see what fish were really in the sea. And if they were ones I would keep on the hook or throw back with a gentle "I'm sorry but I met someone else" response or a "No, thank you, I'm not interested in partner swapping" answer. Maybe I ought to change my erotica answer.

I love not having to sit in a smoke-filled bar or on an exercise bike at the gym to find Mr. Right! I can chat, right in the comfort of my own home, in my sweats and no makeup before I decide if he seems worthy of wrestling into a pair of pantyhose for. After the forty question test, a criminal background check and a drive-by of his house to see if he's legit and there really is no Mrs., I've got myself a date.

Lo and behold, there he was. Nice Guy Looking for Ms. Right! He brought me flowers, sat close, was attentive and flirted like a gentleman without crossing the line. Six hours later he gave me goose bumps by whispering in my ear, politely asking if he could kiss me goodnight and could he see me tomorrow. The clock struck midnight. I ran out dramatically, leaving my shoe behind. Cinderella was a smart girl teaching us the leave-behind method. All I can say is the rest is history. We're a product of cyberspace dating and can attest to it being just as romantic and successful as many other methods. Blind, drunk or otherwise!

I have had two previous harrowing relationships that tested every moral fiber in my DNA. They caused me to examine who I am as a woman, partner and mother. They taught me to understand not only what I believe in but more importantly what I will not tolerate. Love should never hurt! Nor require so much hard work it consumes me. Due to my past indiscretions which almost shattered my faith in the male species, I have grown immensely; that passive girl has blossomed into a secure and mature woman who now knows what she wants. I deserve love and happiness and won't hesitate to seek it out. I am finally smart enough to hang onto a great guy for the treasure he is but also clever enough to dismiss him if he isn't suitable or is a total rehab project!

I am confident I have found real and true love. It's like being home and there's no place like it! (No, wait, that's Dorothy's line!) There's a feeling of such comfortableness, as if we have been friends all of our lives. My loyal prince consistently makes me feel safe and grounded. He is a genuine soul mate who has infused joy and laughter into my life and surrounds me with contentment. My handsome knight showers me with tender affection, passion, understanding and support. He has befriended and fathered my children despite the absence of biological duty. Along with him, his package deal includes two more wonderful (testosterone filled) sons.

Kris (my Clyde) is my happy place and I will share my happily ever after with him for a long time. As much as I love him, though, if I ever peer into the mirror and witness the startling revelation of a resemblance between us, the candlestick maker might just have to go!

CHAPTER 24

Nine Days' Grace after the Milk Expires

Memory is an amazing capacity we all have. We could hardly exist without the ability to remember that we got oil for the lawn mower yesterday, changed our bedding and rotated our fleet of mattresses today and that we have to defrost the pot roast for a dinner party tomorrow. Being a mother means we have to compound the amount of information we'll have to recollect by the number of kids we produced. The equation is mind-boggling and the task is a daily challenge of immense proportion.

We get little credit for all of the trillions of items remembered, such as invitation RSVPs, appointments, medicine schedules, repairs, meal planning, car maintenance, vacation arrangements, pet feedings, homework assignments, payment due dates, hygiene, entertainment coordinating, chores, movie rentals and laundry.

Looking in my purse provides a whole litany of items I did remember. A Nuk, a blue crayon, an appointment calendar with scribbles on every page, a piece of broken shoelace to repair, a rare moth specimen (to complete our collection) pressed between immunization records and some loose pages of a nursery rhyme book, a half-chewed and soggy teething cookie, a deck of Old Maid cards, a grocery list (with discarded chewing gum folded under the corner), small damp socks rolled in a ball, Matchbox® car, Band-Aid wrapper, an inhaler, slightly brown slices of apple, sunblock, semi-moist wipes, aspirin, a baggie of Cheerios, a diaper, beads from a broken necklace scattered about, packet of powder drink mix and a collapsible cup, library cards, antacid tablets, used tissues and needle and thread for mending. Now, where are my damn car keys?

I remembered the umbrella, extra pair of dry underwear, batteries and marshmallows for the campout. Who needs firewood?

I remembered to paint my second-grader's race car at 11 p.m. the night before the Cub Scouts pinewood derby so that he could participate. Maybe I should have warned the referee that the paint was still wet?

I faithfully packed thousands of lunches and dipped into my change jar countless times to retrieve milk money, field trip money, and last-minute book club fees. But the one time I forgot to send a lunch on the zoo field trip I was ostracized. He's lucky I had sent some change along. At least he could fetch some high-protein goat pellets out of the vending machine to tide him over.

I bought all the supplies for the modeling-clay landforms diorama with only loose change and a day's notice (which came to me on a sticky note that was precariously stuck to the inside of my child's jacket sleeve). I couldn't help it that the only color of clay left on the store shelf was purple.

I remembered every birthday with a cake, gift and party, even when at the end of each previous chaotic birthday celebration I swore I would never do it again. Unfortunately September is a popular month and the Little Mermaid cake was the only one left. Maybe it wasn't an ideal theme for a boy's ten-year-old birthday party and I feel bad that now my son's nickname is Ariel but a little embarrassment helps to build character. Someday he may thank me.

Over the years it was me who remembered to feed the two hamsters, guinea pig, turtle, three cats, hermit crab, hundreds of aquatic specimens including a puffer-fish, two dogs, multiple rabbits and many adopted strays. It's not that I forgot to feed the snakes, I refused. They died.

I remembered to make everyone's favorite meals for a celebration and treats for a reward. Nicole loves lasagna and Ryan loves chicken. No, wait. Maybe it's the other way around. Brad got a box of chocolate-covered cherries every Christmas season because I knew he'd be delighted and I often remembered to treat Alex to a kiddie cone just because he loved them so much. Not to mention I had to first slip him lactose pills that I carried in my purse for easy access, so he wouldn't end up on the toilet in seven minutes flat from intestinal bloating. I remembered to do that ritual all but twice. Once he missed a first-grade Thanksgiving reenactment play and the second time he missed two innings of a softball game because of it. There will be plenty of other games to make up for it and I assure you the part of the pilgrim will be available next year too.

I recall I had to hide a couple of forgotten teeth under their pillows so they could be rewarded by the tooth fairy; which I also remembered. I did forget to get change for a ten-dollar bill once so the payout was extra generous. (She never even got a thank you.)

Once, I confess, Saint Nick was a day late but after I showed my kids a dead deer nearby on the side of the road and explained that he couldn't continue his route without a full team, it all made sense to them.

I reminded my kids to wear clean underwear to doctor visits, brush their teeth before dental checkups and clean their ears prior to hearing tests at school. Although I suppose those reminders were more for saving my reputation than theirs.

I never missed a clarinet rental payment, grueling band concert or a soccer game (even during their losing 0-8 season). I was present at countless Cub Scouts meetings, Little League games, gymnastics practices and dance recitals. But the one time I forgot to pick my son up from summer day camp he wanted to call social services.

I remembered to fluff my daughter's cashmere sweater in the dryer for precisely six minutes so it wouldn't shrink, pay to dry-clean her suede skirt (which cost more than the skirt itself) and purposefully stretch the sleeves on her green shirt to fit. Yet she was so angry and nearly wet herself once because she couldn't get her pants off at school. It appears my quick, superb mending job on the zipper of her pants while she was waiting for the bus that morning was a bit too secure. We had to cut them off of her when she got home.

I did remember to teach my offspring valuable pieces of information too. Stop! You can't dry a wet bunny in the microwave. I proved that tree limbs smaller than your leg won't hold your weight. Read the whole magician's manual before you attempt to saw your sister in half. You can hem pants with a glue gun. Riding your bike with a flat tire will bend the rim. And I insisted that when we get separated in a public place they shouldn't wander around looking for me. I instructed them to stay put in one spot and wait for me to come back to find them.

Some things I didn't really forget to tell them because they figured them out on their own. Such as the fact that corn doesn't digest well and, like magical clockwork, you will see it again fourteen hours after you eat it. Tripping on your shoelace can cause injury and embarrassment. If you eat seven cups of butterscotch pudding in a contest, the bet should be higher than $9 to make it worthwhile. If someone asks you to put out your arm so they can give you a snake bite, say no. Crying over spilt milk can relieve stress so let Mommy alone while she is doing it. And if you eat too much soap it gives you diarrhea.

Some of the tenets I taught them have been dispelled over time. None of their eyes blew out of their sockets by holding them open while sneezing. Their mouths didn't stretch out by putting their fists in them. (However, a foot-in-the-mouth is a different story.) They proved they can cross the street and not get hit without me holding their hand and that falling off a trampoline and landing on your head does hurt but doesn't always break your neck. One of my smarty pants even ran with a scissor and lived to tell about it. What a rebel.

There's stuff that I didn't coach my kids about for obvious reasons. After it was too late, then I reconsidered. I wish I had remembered to teach my teenager that if she leaves the scene of an accident unnoticed after hitting a bridge, don't leave your license plate behind as evidence. People are usually friends with compatible intelligence, so if they're going to cheat on a test, choose an upperclassman. It might be okay to lie if you are at a pay-according-to-your-weight buffet or if anyone asks if I dye my hair. Finally, don't hand out my phone number and try to fix me up on a date with your male principal, teachers or janitor. Well, I might make an exception for Mr. Johnson the gym teacher.

This is a dedication and a thank you to all of the moms who scribbled their child's name on valentines for classmates at 10 p.m. on February 13th, picked up next year's Christmas gift exchange item at a rummage sale (and cleaned it up so that it's wrapped and ready) and brought popcorn snacks for the whole gymnastics class even if the individual servings came in cut-down Wal-Mart bags with zip ties on top. It's the thought that counts!

I sure am grateful you remembered to instruct your kids how to use a plunger. I appreciate that your kids listen to me (better than my own in fact) when I insist they don't stick things up their nose. You remembered to teach them manners which included a thank you for a ride to the emergency room.

I just remembered that I have a bottle of whiskey so I propose a toast to all of the women who successfully keep their households functioning smoothly. Aside from an occasional memory warp they have gotten their kids delivered to and safely retrieved from all of their destinations; appointments have been kept; and all educational requirements have been met. You deserve a pat on the back for achievement, a medal of honor for your dedication, a cake that you don't have to share with anyone and a hangover in remembrance.

You go on and celebrate without me. I'll catch up later. My dinner is almost done and I have to run and take care of a few things before I put the rolls in the oven. The milk is ten days past expiration so I'll pick some up at the gas station on the way to the vet for the cats' shots and get back to the post office before they close at 5 p.m. Now that I think of it, the last place I saw Alex, he was trying on shoes—I better hurry back to Kohl's Department Store to find him!

Once a mom, always a mom!

ACKNOWLEDGEMENTS

I thank this list of superbly talented women for whom I am grateful, for their vast expertise, great support and warm encouragement.

Nancy Cleary, CEO of Wyatt-MacKenzie Publishing,
www.wyattmackenzie.com

Lisa Pliscou, Editor

Mahalia Sobhani, Editing,
Brookfield, WI

Kat Hustedde, Illustrator,
www.kathustedde.com

Iris Waichler, Author of: *Riding the Infertility Roller Coaster, A Guide to Educate and Inspire*, www.infertilityrollercoaster.com

Attorney Lisa Vanden Heuvel,
www.vhdlaw.com

Julie Watson Smith, Author of: *Mommyhood Diaries,*
www.juliewatsonsmith.com

Dr. Marna Moolla,
www.drmarnamoolla.com

ABOUT THE AUTHOR

As a comedienne in the past, Bonnie used to perform her relatable and comedic stories for many years. Due to the challenging logistics of going out to comedy clubs with four kids at home, Bonnie took to writing and has compiled her heartfelt, candid and laughable observations so she could bring them to her audience in a new medium. She is a member of the National Writers Union, Wisconsin Speakers Association and has had a few entries published in the Milwaukee Journal Sentinel. Bonnie grew up in Cedarburg, WI and now resides in Slinger, WI with two of her boys. This old woman who lives in a shoe… continues writing about her zany world and enjoys speaking engagements to share her humor and encouragement to mothers of all ages.

www.maternallyspeaking.com

Download your OVARIAN CLUB CERTIFICATE
in full color at:

www.tinyurl.com/ovarianclubcertificate

The President and Fellow Members of the

Ovarian Club

Rewards this Certificate of Hormonal Excellence to

Superwoman

A D D   D E S E R V I N G   N A M E

You deserve a pat on the back for achievement, a medal of honor for your dedication, a cake you don't have to share with anyone, and a hangover in remembrance.

Beth Feldkamp

NEW MEMBER

Bonnie Zewell

PRESIDENT

LaVergne, TN USA
06 April 2010
178175LV00005B/1/P